William Shakespeare's

The Merchant of Venice

The Novel

Shakespeare's Classic Play Retold As a Novel

Retold By Thomas Flesh

BookCaps™ Study Guides

www.SwipeSpeare.com

Table of Contents

About This Series

This book is part of an expanding series that retells Shakespeare into fiction. If you'd like to be notified when the next book is available, visit:

http://www.swipespeare.com/mailing-list.html

If you enjoy this series, check out our Shakespeare iPhone / iPad / Android / Windows app: SwipeSpeare. It puts all of Shakespeare's plays into modern English with the swipe of a finger!

Part One

Chapter 1

The streets of Venice bustled with people. The spring weather had struck the rare balance of warm while managing to avoid being too humid- a miracle of a sort for a city surrounded and cut through with water.

Since Antonio had no important meetings that day, he had decided to close down his trading company's office for a bit and join most of Venice in walking about. Along the way, he ran into Salarino and Salanio, two friends who joined him. As they walked and talked, the conversation turned to Antonio's mood.

"I have no idea why I am so sad," he said. "It tires me and you say it tires you, too. And how I came about being so sad-- whatever it's about and where it comes from-- I do not know. It all makes me feel so stupid, and I have to make it my business to know myself."

“You’re thinking about the ocean and wondering how your ships are doing,” said Salarino very matter of factually. “They are fine, like citizens on the deep waves or like a play out on the sea— they are large and look down on the smaller ships that bow to them and pay them respects as they fly past with their elegant sails.”

“Trust me, if I had dealings going on like you do most all of my thoughts and attention would be on the business overseas,” Salanio agreed. “I would be plucking up blades of grass to figure out which way the wind blows and peering at maps looking for ports and piers and roads. Any little thing that might make me afraid of bad luck taking over my business would fill me with doubt and that would make me sad.”

"Blowing on my soup to cool it would make me feel so upset because I'd think of the harm a strong wind at sea might do to my ships," Salarino continued. "I wouldn't be able to look at sand in an hourglass without worrying about shallow waters with sandbars. I'd see my majestic ship Andrew docked in the sand, upside down with the sails in the water sinking to her death. If I were to go to church I'd see the stones it is made of and I couldn't help but think of dangerous rocks which could split the sides of my ship, scattering all the spices in the hold into the ocean and tossing the silks inside upon the waves. In an instant- It'd be worth nothing." Salarino snapped his fingers for emphasis at that last thought. "How could I have these thoughts about all that could go wrong and not worry? The things I'd imagine that could happen would make me so sad. You don't have to tell me—I know, Antonio is sad to think of all that could happen to his merchandise."

Antonio shook his head at his friends' speculating. "No, trust me, that's not it. I am financially stable and I don't have everything invested in one ship or in one place. My finances are not dependent on how well I do this year, so it's not the merchandise in the ships making me sad."

"Well, then, you must be in love," said Salarino with a surety that made Antonio laugh.

"Get out of here!" said Antonio with a chuckle.

“Not in love, either?” asked Salarino with a smile. “Well let’s just say you are sad because you are not happy. It would be just as easy for you to laugh and dance and say you are happy because you are not sad. Humans have two faces and many people have strange ways of expressing moods. Some will look out at the world and laugh at just about anything while others are so sour and bitter they won’t ever crack a smile, even at the funniest jokes in the world.”

“Here comes your cousin Bassanio, along with Gratiano and Lorenzo,” said Salanio. He motioned his head down the street where the three young men were approaching. Bassanio waved his hand and Antonio waved back. “We’ll see you later- they’ll be better company for you.”

“I would have stayed until I cheered you up if friends you are closer to hadn’t shown up,” said Salarino

“You are worth much to me in that way,” said Antonio. “I’m thinking your own business needs you and you are taking the chance to leave.”

“Hello, my good men!” said Salarino.

“Hello, both of you,” said Bassanio. “When will we get together for fun? When? I never see you these days. Does it have to be that way?”

"We'll be available whenever you want to get together," responded Salarino. He and Salanio shook hands and walked off, leaving Antonio with new company.

"Bassanio, since you have found Antonio, we will go ahead," said Lorenzo. "But at dinner time don't forget we're getting together."

"No problem, I'll be there," said Bassanio.

Not taking the cue to leave Gratiano began speaking. "You don't look so good, Antonio. You take the world too seriously. You don't gain anything by investing so much. Trust me, you don't seem quite yourself."

"The world is just the world, Gratiano," responded Antonio. "A stage where every man must play a part, and mine is a sad one."

"Well then let me play the fool's part." Gratiano became excited at the chance to spout some thoughts he had been mulling over earlier. "I will have fun and laugh until I am wrinkled. And let me ruin my liver with wine rather than my heart be ruined with crying. Why should a man whose blood is warm sit still like the statue of his grandfather carved in stone? Why should he sleep when he is awake and grow sickly from being irritable? I'll tell you what, Antonio- I love you, and it is my love that speaks when I say there is a type of man whose face becomes frothy and scummy like a stagnant pond, who is purposely silent and still, to try to make others see them as wise, respected and important, as if they are saying 'I am Mr. Wiseman, and when I open my mouth, dogs should stop barking!' Antonio, I know of many men who are thought to be very wise simply by saying nothing, but I'm sure if they were to speak, it would be painful to hear and those hearing them would see them as fools."

Glancing at Lorenzo, Gratiano finally understood that he was overstaying his welcome. "I'll talk more about this some other time. But for now, stop looking for sadness It's foolish to do so, in my opinion. Come on, Lorenzo, let's go. I'll say more about this after dinner."

“Well, we will see you at dinner time,” Lorenzo as he shook Bassanio's hand and started walking away. “I must be one of these dumb wise men because Gratiano never lets me speak.”

“Well, hang out with me for another couple of years and you won’t even recognize the sound of your own voice.”

“See you later. I’ll become a talker after all of this!” said Antonio.

“Thanks, and trust me, silence is only good in a cow’s tongue that’s ready to eat or that of an old maid.”

Left alone, Antonio turned to Bassanio. “Is that important what he says?”

Bassanio shrugged his shoulders. “Gratiano says a lot about nothing- more than any other man in Venice. The point he tries to make is like two grains of wheat hidden in a haystack: you spend the whole day looking for them and once you find them, you realize they weren’t worth the trouble.”

Antonio smiled at the answer. He could see in Bassanio's young eyes his close friend, who had died more than a decade ago, followed soon by his wife. This tragedy solidified the relationship between Antonio and the orphaned Bassanio, which moved between that of father and son to brothers depending on moods and context. Right now it was the former, as Antonio had heard word of what Bassanio was up to.

“So, tell me now who is the girl you’re taking a secret trip to see? The one you promised to tell me about today?”

“Well, as you know, Antonio I’ve more or less ruined my finances by living the high life and spending way beyond my means.”

Antonio knew very well. As Bassanio had no close relations to speak of, the tidy fortune that his father had left him was quickly spent, as one left to an unsupervised young man in Venice was bound to be.

“I’m not complaining about having to cut back from what I was used to spending,” Bassanio continued “and my main concern is to be able to pay off all of the debts that all that time of extravagant overspending left me with. To you, Antonio, I owe the most, in both money and appreciation, and because of your kindness I feel it is my duty to share with you my plan for clearing myself of the debts I owe.”

Antonio had never expected Bassanio to pay him back, as he had given the money out of love. It was Bassanio who had kept a close account of what he took from Antonio, grateful for it. "Please, Bassanio, tell me your plan and if it sounds solid, as you yourself do, on my word, you can be certain that my money, myself and anything I can do for you are at your disposal to help you."

"Back when I was in school, if I lost an arrow I would shoot another one in the same direction in the exact same way, but I'd watch it closer in order to find the first one, and by shooting both I found both, most of the time. I tell you this story because what I'm about to say may sound silly. I owe you a lot, and like a stubborn child, I lost everything I owe you. But if you are willing to shoot another arrow in the same direction as the first one you shot for me, I have no doubt I will watch where it goes and find both or, at the very least, bring the second one back and only owe you for the first."

"You know me well, and you are spending too much time going on about our friendship with such detail," said Antonio. "You're doing more harm by doubting our friendship and making me wonder about us now than if you had destroyed all that I have. Just tell me what it is you need me to do and as long as you know I am capable of doing it, I will do it. So, just tell me what you need."

"In Belmont there is a woman who has inherited a lot of money and she is beautiful, and even better than that, she is a good person. Sometimes the way she looks at me makes me think she is trying to let me know she likes me. Her name is Portia, and she is no less valuable than the Portia who is Cato's daughter and married to Brutus. The whole world knows how wealthy she is and the four winds from every direction blow in famous suitors, and her blond hair falls in her face like the golden fleece in the Greek myth, and her estate on the coast of Belmont is like Colchos, and many men come to win her, like Jason in the myth. Antonio, if I only had the money to hold my own against them, I know in my mind I could win her heart and I have no doubt I'd be successful!"

"You know that all my money is invested in my ships and I don't have the money on hand or the goods to raise the cash you need." Antonio waited a beat before continuing. "So, let's go and see what my good credit in Venice can drum up. We'll get as big a loan as possible to provide what you need to get to Belmont and beautiful Portia. Go ask around, and so will I, let's find out where the money is and I won't hesitate to sign for it in my name."

Chapter 2

Portia sat at a window, looking out on her large estate in Belmont. The sun was shining and the air was crisp with the smell of spring flowers. Were the state of the weather to be determined by Portia's expression and demeanor though, one would think that Belmont was in the midst of an extended storm.

“My word, but my little body is so tired of this big world,” Portia sighed.

“You would be tired, as well,” Nerissa said, “if your troubles were in the same proportion as your fortunes are, and yet, from what I see, people who have too much get as sick from having too much as those who starve and have nothing. It is no small happiness, therefore, to be right in the middle: having too much ages one faster, while having just enough extends your life.”

“True words, and well spoken,” Portia told her maid and friend who was sewing in the corner.

“They would be even better if you followed them.”

"If it were as easy to do as it is to know what good to do, small chapels would be great churches and poor men's cottages would become prince's palaces. It is a good priest who follows his own instructions: I can easier teach twenty people of the good that can be done than be one of the twenty to follow my own teaching. The brain can come up with laws for the blood, but a hot temper overtakes a well-thought out decision: just like a rabbit, young people jump over the nets of good advice held by crippled old men. But thinking in this way is not the sort that will help choose a husband. Oh, my! The word 'choose!' I can not choose who I'd like or refuse who I don't like; such is the fate of a living daughter restricted by the wishes of a dead father. It's hard, isn't it, Nerissa, that I can't choose one or refuse any?"

"Your father was a good man, and religious men at their death sometimes have well-intentioned ideas, and that's why we have the lottery he came up with using these three trunks of gold, silver and lead, where whoever can figure out the right answer chooses you and the trunk won't, don't doubt it, be chosen by any except the one who is right for you. But are you having warm feelings toward any of these princely suitors that have already arrived?"

"I'll tell you what—go over their names, and as you name them, I will describe them, and according to my description you will be able to guess how I feel about them."

Nerissa put down her work and took a minute to arrange the names in her head. “First, there is the Neapolitan prince.”

“Yes, now there’s a foolish youth, for sure, who does nothing but talk about his horse, and he makes a big deal that he has the unique ability of being able to shoe the horse himself. I very much fear the woman who is his mother had an affair with a blacksmith.”

“Next is the Count Palatine.”

“He does nothing but frown, as if to say ‘If you do not choose me, I do not care.’ He hears happy stories and does not smile at them: I suspect he will be the sad philosopher when he grows old since he is so full of inappropriate sadness in his youth. I would rather be married to a skull with a bone in it mouth than to either of these. God forbid I end up with one of them!”

“What do you think about the French lord, Monsieur Le Bon?”

“God made him so let’s call him a man. Truth be told, I know it is a sin to make fun of people, but him! He has a horse better than the prince for Naples and a better way of frowning than the Count Palatine; he is every man you’d want in no man. If a bird begins to sing, he begins to prance; he will fence with his own shadow to show off. If I were to marry him I would marry twenty husbands. It he were to hate me I would forgive him, and if he were to love me to madness, I would never give him the same love.”

“Well, what do you say about Falconbridge, the young baron of England?”

“I really have nothing to say about him because he does not understand me, and I don’t understand him. He doesn’t speak Latin, French, or Italian, and anyone in the court knows I don’t know English of any value at all. He’s really good looking, but who can talk with someone who doesn’t understand them? And he was dressed so weirdly! He must have bought his jacket in Italy, his tights in France, his hat in Germany and his way of behaving everywhere.”

“What do you think of his neighbor, the Scottish lord?”

"I think he has a neighborly generosity about him, because he took a slap to the ear by the Englishman and swore he would pay him back as soon as he was able. I think the Frenchman guaranteed he would help the Scotsman and then added a slap of his own."

"How do you like the young German, the Duke of Saxony's nephew?"

"He's pretty wretched in the morning, when he is sober, and even more so in the afternoon, when he is drunk. When he is best, he is a little worse than a man, and when he is worst, he is not much better than an animal. If he were to die, I would think I could do okay without him."

"If he wants to try and choose and he chooses the right box, you would be refusing to go by what your father wants if you were to refuse to marry him."

"I know, so for fear of the worst, let me ask you to place a huge glass of German white wine on the wrong box so that even if it is the wrong one he will be tempted by the wine and I know he would choose it. I will do anything, Nerissa, before I marry a drunk."

"You don't have to worry about having any of these suitors: they have all told me their decision is to, indeed, return to their home and to not try to win you unless you may be won in some other way than your father's command that they choose the correct box."

Portia stood up from her seat at the window and walked over to her dresser, where stood a small, clam shell frame. One side had a portrait of her mother, the other of her father; they were both quite young when this was painted. She took it and stared at them. "If I live to be as old as Sibylla, I will die an old maid unless I am won in the manner my father has willed. I am glad this group of wooers is so reasonable as to leave because there is not one of them I care about except for their absence, so I wish them all a good departure."

"Do you remember when your father was alive, a Venetian—a scholar and a soldier—who came here in the company of the Marquis of Montferrat?"

"Yes, yes I do. That was Bassanio, at least I think that was his name."

"Yes, madam: he, of all the men that I've ever laid eyes on, was the best and deserving of a beautiful woman."

“I remember him well, and I recall him being worthy of your praise.” A servant entered the room. “What is it? What is the news?”

“There are four strangers here for you, madam,” the servant said. “They want to say goodbye and there is a messenger coming from a fifth, the Prince of Morocco, who brings news that the prince, his master, will be here tonight.”

“If I could say hello to the fifth with as much enthusiasm as I say goodbye to the other four, I would be glad of his arrival. Ff he is like a saint but looks like a devil I would rather he would forgive me rather than marry me. Come on, Nerissa. Sir, go ahead. While we shut the gates upon one wooer, another one knocks at the door.”

Portia and Nerissa followed the servant out of the room.

Chapter 3

Shylock ambled through the streets of Venice, not too far from the ghetto. Even though the weather would've allowed for lighter clothing, he wore the same black cloak he wore most everyday as well as the red cap required of him that identified him as a Jew. Next to him walked Bassanio.

“Three thousand ducats?” asked Shylock.

“Yes, sir, for three months,” answered Bassanio.

“For three months? Well, let’s see.”

“The amount of which, as I told you, Antonio will guarantee to pay.”

“Antonio will guarantee it? Well, let’s see.”

“Will you help me? Will you gratify me? Can I know your answer?”

“Three thousand ducats for three months and Antonio will guarantee it.”

Bassanio was growing impatient of Shylock's repetitions. Wanting an answer to know if he was to move onto another lender. “What is your answer?”

"Antonio is a good man."

"Have you heard anyone say anything to contradict that?"

"Oh. No, no, no, no. What I meant when I said he is a good man is that I am saying he is sufficient." Shylock turned around. He didn't want to be caught outside of the ghetto's locked gates when evening came and wanted to stay close. "Even though his investments are tied up: he has a ship on its way to Tripolis and another headed toward the Indies. I also understand, from people at Rialto, he has a third ship at Mexico, a fourth bound for England, and many other business ventures abroad on the seas. But ships are just made of wood, and sailors are men. There are land rats and water rats, water thieves and land thieves. I mean pirates, and then there is the danger of the waters, winds and rocks. The man, despite all of this, has money. Three thousand ducats, I think I will let him guarantee it."

"You can be certain you can."

"I will be certain I can, and so that I might be certain, I'll think of a way. May I speak with Antonio?"

"You are welcome to join us for dinner."

"What, and smell pork? To eat of the sort of animal which your prophet Jesus charmed the devil into? I will buy with you, sell with you, talk with you, walk with you, and so on, but I will not eat with you, drink with you, or pray with you."

By complete luck, Antonio crossed Bassanio's vision at that moment. "There he is now!" he said, and ran down the street after him to bring him to Shylock.

From a distance, Shylock saw Antonio clearly. "He looks just like a gloating tax collector!" he thought to himself. "I hate him because he is a Christian. But more so because he foolishly lends out money with no interest and brings down the rate of interest for us here in Venice. If I can just get him into an unfavorable position just once, I will satisfy the old grudge I have against him. He hates our sacred nation and he rants in the places where the merchants gather about me, and my deals and my well-earned profit that he refers to as interest. Jews everywhere would be cursed if I were to forgive him."

Bassanio brought Antonio over. Shylock spoke when they were both near. "I am thinking about how much I have on hand, and, if my memory serves me right, I can't instantly come up with the total ff the full three thousand ducats. But so what? Tubal, a wealthy Jew I know will give it to me. But wait! How many months did you say you need it?" Shylock nodded his head towards Antonio. "How are you, signior? We were just talking about you."

“Shylock, although I generally never lend or borrow by charging or paying interest,” Antonio said, “but in order to help supply my friend’s needs I will do it this time. Does he know yet how much it is you need?”

“Oh, yes, three thousand ducats,” said Shylock.

“For three months,” added Bassanio.
“I had forgotten—three months. You told me that. Well, then, your loan. Well, let me see. But, listen, I thought you said you never lend or borrow with interest?”

“I don’t,” affirmed Antonio.

“When Jacob looked after his uncle Laban’s sheep— Jacob, by the way, was Abram’s grandson, and his mother had set it up to his advantage that he would be heir to Abram, yes, third in line--”

“What’s your point about him? Did he take interest?” Antonio's dislike of the Jewish people was piqued by this man speaking about characters from the Old Testament and he grew impatient.

“No, he did not take interest, not, as you would say, direct interest, anyway. Listen, here is what he did: at the time Laban and Jacob agreed that all the baby lambs that were multicolored would be Jacob’s pay. The females were ready to breed since it was the end of autumn, and turning to the males. While the sheep were in the act of breeding, Jacob cut and peeled multicolored pieces of wood and while the sheep were mating he stuck the wood pieces in the ground in front of the females so that they would see them while conceiving and then bear multicolored babies, which went to Jacob. This was a way to be successful and he was blessed. Profit is a blessing as long as you don’t steal it.”

“That was a business deal that Jacob worked for. It was not in his power to make it happen, it was influenced by the God’s will. Are you telling this story to justify charging interest? Are you comparing your gold and silver to breeding sheep?”

“I can’t tell the difference. It multiplies just as fast. But listen to me, signior--”

“Pay attention to this, Bassanio,” Antonio interrupted Shylock. “The devil can cite Scripture to suit his purpose. An evil person who brings out holy evidence is like a villain who smiles at you. A seemingly good apple can be rotten at the core and a seemingly honest appearance can hide lies!”

Everything became quiet between the three of them. Bassanio felt some tension between the two older men that felt stronger than what should have resulted from just asking for a large amount of money.

After what seemed like minutes, Shylock spoke. “Three thousand ducats. That’s a good round amount. Three months out of twelve, well, let me see. The rate--”

“Well, Shylock, will you lend us the money?”

“Signior Antonio, you have often, many times, judged my behavior in the Rialto regarding how I use my money to earn interest. I have taken all of this with great patience, for suffering is just what Jews do. You call me a heretic, a murderous dog, and spit upon my Jewish cloak. All because I’m doing what I want with what is mine. Well, now it seems you need my help. All right, then. So, you come to me and you say ‘Shylock, we need some money.’ You ask me for it. You, who spit on my beard And kicked me just like you would kick a stray dog out the door. Here you are now asking for money. So, should I bow to you and in a slave-like tone, holding my breath and whispering humbly, say ‘Oh, good sir, you spit on me last Wednesday and scorned me another day and another time called me a dog, and because of these gestures of respect I’ll lend you as much money as you need?’”

“I’m likely to call you a dog again, and to spit on you again, and to scorn you, too. If you lend us the money, don’t lend it like you would to friends. For since when do friends expect the coins of his friend to reproduce for him? Instead, lend it as if you were lending it to an enemy, who—if he goes broke—you can more easily punish.”

“Well, look at how upset you are getting! I want to be friends with you and get along. I can forget all of the shameful things you’ve done to me and lend you the money without taking interest for the use of it. But you’ll not hear this kind offer I make.”

“It would be kind,” Bassanio said. As soon as he had spoken up, he regretted it. Both of the older men turned to him and delivered harsh stares. Bassanio regretted asking Shylock for the loan, as he had clearly created friction with a history that was beyond his knowledge.

“I can show this kindness,” Shylock spoke. “Go with me to a notary and let’s seal your loan without interest. Then, for a joke, let’s write in that if you don’t pay me on a particular day, at a particular location all of the money I lend to you, let it be said that you will give me as a penalty an exact pound of your flesh, which will be cut off and taken from whatever part of your body I want.”

Antonio recognized the offer for what it was: an insult and challenge. Were he of calmer temper, he might have just walked away and taken the time to find another lender tomorrow, as his good standing in the Christian Venetian community would have easily gotten him the loan. But he was angry, and thus accepted the terms. “I'll accept that in good faith. I'll sign the bond and even say that Jews are very kind.”

Bassanio was shocked. “I will not let you sign such a loan for me. I'd rather go without the money.”

“Don't worry about it. I won't forfeit it. Within the next two months, which is a month before the amount is due, I expect profits of three times the amount of this loan.”

“Oh, father Abram, what kind of people these Christians are whose own ways of dealing taught them to suspect the intentions of others!” Shylock said. “Please, just tell me this: If he should not have the money on time, what could I possibly gain by taking a pound of his flesh for the forfeit? A pound of a man's flesh taken from his body ts not worth very much—it's not even worth as much as the flesh of lambs, cows or goats. I'm saying to win his esteem, I am offering this friendship. If he will take it, good. If not, then goodbye. And please don't slander me for making the offer.”

“Yes, Shylock, I will sign for the loan by your terms.”

“Then meet me at the notary’s give him the details of our little joke. I will go and get the money right away, first I have to check on my house—I left it under the care of a useless servant. After that I will meet up with you.”

“Hurry up, my kind Jewish friend,” Antonio sneered as Shylock left with a wave of his hand. “The Jew is almost Christian, he’s being so kind.”

“I don’t like pretty ways from someone with the mind of a villain,” Bassanio said.

“Come on, there’s no need to worry. My ships return a month before the day the loan is due.”

Part Two

Chapter 1

In the entrance hall of Portia's house, the sound of trumpets piped up, announcing an entrance. Portia stood with Nerissa and some attendants as the Prince of Morocco entered with a train of servants. After bowing to Portia and kissing her hand, he spoke up.

"Please don't dislike me for my skin color. The sun has made my skin so dark since I was born under it and lived near it. Show me the palest skinned man that was born in northern regions, where the sun's warmth barely thaws the icicles, and I will make a cut in my skin to prove my blood is just as red as his. I can tell you that the darkness of my skin has made brave men fear me and I swear to you the finest young women in my region have loved it. I would not change my color except to find a place in your thoughts, gentle queen."

“I am not led in my choice of a husband based solely on how good looking a man is to the ladies,” Portia said. “Besides, the contest with the trunks my father devised takes away my right to freely choose. But if my father had not robbed me of choosing, and restricted me with his cleverness, I'd give myself as wife to any man who wins me fairly, and you, famous prince, would stand as much a chance as any other suitor I have already met of winning my heart.”

“For that, I thank you. So, please lead me to the trunks to try my luck. By this sword that killed the Sophy and a Persian prince, that won three battles with Sultan Solyman, I would out-stare the meanest eyes in the world and act braver than the most daring man on earth. I'd take a mother bear's cubs from her, and would even tease a roaring, hungry lion to win your love, lady. But, this is not good! If Hercules and Lichas were to toss dice to decide which is the better man, the best toss may by a turn of luck come from the weaker hand. Just as Alcides could be beaten by his servant, I might also, led by blind luck, miss the opportunity for you that one less worthy might win and I would die with grief about it.”

“You must take your chance, and either choose not to attempt it at all or swear before choosing that if you choose wrong you will never speak to any lady again about marriage. That's the deal.”

“I won't get married if I lose. So, let me take my chance.”

“Let’s go to the temple first. After dinner you can make your guess.”

“I’ll hope for good fortune! I will be the luckiest man or the most cursed man in the world.”

Chapter 2

Shylock's servant Launcelot wandered some blocks away from his work, talking to himself. “I'm certain I will feel guilty if I run away from this Jew who is my master. But the devil is at my side and tempts me by saying ‘Gobbo, Launcelot Gobbo, good Launcelot,’ or ‘good Gobbo,’ or ‘good Launcelot Gobbo, use your legs and take off and run away.’ My conscience says, ‘No, be careful,’ honest Launcelot, be careful, honest Gobbo, or, as I said before, ‘honest Launcelot Gobbo, do not run, hold your heels.’ But, not to be deterred, the devil tells me to pack it up. ‘Hurry up!’ says the devil. ‘Let's go!’ says the devil. ‘For God's sake, be brave, says the devil, ‘and run.’ Well, my conscience, which hangs close to my heart, says very wisely to me, ‘My honest friend Launcelot, you are an honest man's son.’ Or, rather, an honest woman's son, for my father had characteristics, something that was a part of him, a certain kind of taste for cheating. But my conscience says, ‘Launcelot, don't run.’ ‘Run,’ says the devil. ‘Don't run,’ says my conscience. ‘Conscience,’ I say, ‘you give good advice. ‘Devil,’ I say, ‘you give good advice.’ If I go with my conscience, I will stay with my master the Jew, who, to be sure, is a kind of devil. And to run away from the Jew, I will be ruled by the devil, who, forgive me, is the devil himself. Certainly, the Jew is the devil incarnate, and in my conscience, I know my conscience is giving me some hard advice to tell me to stay with the Jew. The devil gives kinder advice: I will run, devil, my heels are at your command, I will run."

It was here- in the midst of Launcelot's rant- that his father appeared. Hearing the voice, he approached him, carrying his basket by his side. "Can you tell me, young man, please, which is the way the master Jew's home?"

"Oh my god," thought Launcelot "it is my real father! And he's more than just a little blind, he's almost totally blind and doesn't recognize me. I'll mess with him a bit."

"Young man, please, can you tell me which way to the master Jew's home?"

"Turn right at the next turn, and then turn left. Immediately, at the next turn, turn neither left nor right, but turn in the direction of the Jew's house."

"My god, it will be hard to find it. Can you tell me whether a man named Launcelot that used to live there still lives there?"

"Do you mean the young Master Launcelot?"

"He's not a master, but a poor man's son. His father, if I might say, is a very honest but poor man and—thank God—will most likely live long."

"Well, let his father be what he will, we are talking about young Master Launcelot."

“I beg your pardon but he is just Launcelot, sir.”

“But I beg you, therefore, old man, I ask you are you talking about young Master Launcelot?”

“I’m talking about Launcelot, yes.”

“Well, then, Master Launcelot. Don’t speak of Master Launcelot, old man, for the young man, according to fate and destiny and other odd reflections, the Three Sisters and those sort of branches of learning, is deceased, or, as one might say in plain terms, he has gone to heaven.”

“By Mary, God forbid! The boy was the very support of my age, he was my prop.”

“Do I look like a short stick or a cane, a staff or a prop? Do you know who I am, old man?”

“I’m sorry, I do not know who you are, young man, but, please, can you tell me, is my son, God rest his soul, alive or dead?”

“You don’t know me, old man?”

“I’m sorry, sir, I am mostly blind.” Old Gobbo pointed to his milky eyes. “I do not know you.”

"No, I think even if you had your sight you wouldn't know me. It is a wise father who can recognize his own child. Well, old man, I will tell you about your son: give me your blessing and the truth will be revealed. A murder cannot be hidden for long. A man's son may be hidden, but eventually the truth will come out."

"Please, sir, stand up. I am sure you are not Launcelot, my son."

"Please, let's not have any more fooling around, just give me your blessing. I am Launcelot, your boy that was, your son that is, your child that will always be."

"I just can't believe you are my son."

"I don't know what to think of that, but I am Launcelot, the Jew's servant, and I am sure that Margery, your wife, is my mother."

"Her name is Margery, yes. I'll be damned, if you are Launcelot, you are my flesh and blood. Praise be to God! What a beard you have got! You have more hair on your chin than my draught horse Dobbin has on his tail."

"It would seem, then that Dobbin's tail grows backward. I am sure he had more hair on his tail than I have on my face last time I saw him."

"God, how you have changed! How do you and your master get along? I've brought him a present." He lifted up the basked he was carrying. "How are you these days?"

"Well, to be honest, as far as I go, I have made up my mind to run away, and I will not rest until I have gained some ground. My master is a Jew. Give him a present! You should give him a noose. I am starving in his service. You can feel every single one of my ribs. Father, I am glad you have come. Give me your present and I will give it to Master Bassanio, who does sometimes give new uniforms. If I can't serve him, I will run as far as God has put ground. Oh, what luck! Here comes the man. Let's go talk to him, father. I will be a Jew if I serve a Jew any longer."

Launcelot took his father and together they walked looking for Bassanio. It was soon after that they managed to find him, talking with his friend Leonardo and some servants.

"Okay, go on," Bassanio directed a servant. "But make sure to do things quickly so that supper is ready no later than five o'clock. Make sure these letters are delivered, and get the uniforms ready, and ask Gratiano to come soon to my home."

"Go to him, father," Launcelot urged Gobbo forward.

"God bless your, sir!" Gobbo said as he stepped in front of Bassanio.

"Thank you!" said Bassanio. "What do you want with me?"

"This is my son, sir, a poor boy-"

Launcelot stepped closer. "Not a poor boy, sir, but the rich Jew's servant, who would, soon, as my father will explain-"

"He very much wants, sir, as one would say, to serve-" said Gobbo.

"Yes, the short and long of it is that I serve the Jew, and I have a desire, as my father will explain-"

"His master and he are, with all respect to you, are hardly good friends-"

"To be brief, the truth is that the Jew, having done me wrong, have caused me, and my father, being, I hope, an old man, will certify for you-"

"I have here a dish of doves that I will give to you, sir," Gobbo lifted his basket "and my request is-"

"In brief, the request is beside the point, as you, sir, will know by this honest old man, and though I say it, though old, yet poor, my father."

Bassanio stepped in to stop their rambling. "Just one of you speak. What do you want?"

“I want to work for you, sir,” said Launcelot.

“That is the heart of the matter, sir,” agreed his father.

“I know who you are,” Bassanio said. “You can have whatever you ask. Your master Shylock spoke with me today and he has recommended you, if you prefer to leave a rich Jew’s service to become the servant of a poor gentleman like me.”

“A familiar old proverb is well split between my master Shylock and you, sir,” said Launcelot. “You have the grace of God, and he has enough.”

“Very well said. Go father, with your son and take leave of your old master and find your way to my house. Give him a uniform more tricked out than the others. See that it’s done.”

"Father, go ahead," Launcelot told Gobbo. "I can't get employment, no. I am not able to talk my way into it. But I doubt any man in Italy has a better palm than I have to swear upon a Bible, and I will have good luck. Look here, here's a simple line of my life, here's a small amount of wives: I'm sorry, fifteen wives is nothing! Eleven widows and nine maids is a simple yield for one man: and to escape drowning twice, and to have my life in danger because I am found in the wrong bed— these are simple escapes. Well, if Fortune is a woman, she's a good girl to give me this stuff. Father, come, I'll leave my Jew in the blink of an eye." Launcelot and Gobbo walked off.

Bassanio directed Leonardo's attention to a crate filled with some food. "Please, good Leonardo, think about this: these are the things to be bought and stored away. Hurry back, I'm having dinner tonight with someone very important. Hurry up, go."

"I'll do my best with this," Leonardo lifted up the crate. As he walked away, he ran into Gratiano.

"Where is your master?"

"He's walking over there," Leonardo nodded his head in the direction of Bassanio.

"Signior Bassanio!"

"Gratiano!"

"I have a favor to ask you."

"It's yours," Bassanio let his good mood shine through.

"You must not say no. I must go with you to Belmont."

"Well, then you must come. But listen to me, Gratiano. Sometimes you are wild—too rude and loud. These things look good on you and do not appear to be faults in my eyes. But where people do not know you, well, those things might see, a bit too unrestrained. So, please, take care to lessen that a bit and add some modesty to your boisterous spirit, to make sure your wild behavior does not reflect badly on me in Belmont and cause me to lose hope of winning Portia."

"Listen to me, Signior Bassanio: If I do not act sober and serious, and talk with respect and only swear occasionally, carry a prayer book with me and appear gentle, even more—if while grace is being said I and I do not cover my eyes with the brim of my hat and quietly say 'amen,' and act civil and polite at all times, like someone deliberately putting on a serious display of manners to please his grandmother, then never trust me again."

"Well, we'll see how you are."

“But tonight doesn’t count. Don’t judge how I will be by how I am tonight.”

“No, that would be a shame. I would rather you be as wild as you can be tonight because our friends will enjoy that and want to have fun. Goodbye for now, I have some things I have to do.”

“And I must get back to Lorenzo and the rest of them. We will see you at dinner.”

Chapter 3

Launcelot had returned to Shylock's house and packed what little he had. Shylock's daughter- Jessica- was there to bid him farewell.

“I’m sorry you are leaving my father’s service,” she said. “This house is hellish and you cheered it up like a funny devil, taking away some small amount of the pain of it all. But, goodbye and take care, here is a ducat for you. Lorenzo, who will be your new master’s guest tonight— please give him this letter. Do it secretly. Well, goodbye. I don’t want my father to see me talking to you.”

“Goodbye! My tears show what I cannot say. Most beautiful pagan, most sweet Jew! A Christian will figure out a way to get you, I have no doubt. But, goodbye. These foolish tears don’t do much to make me appear manly. Goodbye.”

"Goodbye, good Launcelot," she gave him a final, affectionate hug. It surprised him, but he returned it and left the house quickly. It was evident he held no nostalgia for the place. "Oh my god, how terrible am I to be ashamed to be my father's daughter!" Jessica said to herself. "But though I am his daughter by blood, I do not share his behavior. Oh, Lorenzo, if you keep your promise, this will all end and I'll become a Christian and your loving wife."

Chapter 4

“No, we’ll sneak away at dinner time, disguise ourselves at my house and come back within an hour.” Lorenzo turned to Gratiano, Salarino, and Salanio to see what they thought of his plan.

“But we don’t have anything ready,” said Gratiano.

“We haven’t even asked anyone to be torchbearers,” added Salarino.

“It might turn out badly since it’s not well organized. I think it’s best we call it off,” warned Salanio.

“It’s only four o’clock now,” countered Lorenzo. “We have two hours to get it together.”

Launcelot had managed to find Bassanio and received his first task, which he was on his way to do when he ran into Lorenzo and remembered the favor that was asked of him. “How goes it, Launcelot?” asked Lorenzo.

Removing Jessica's letter from his coat, Launcelot handed it to Lorenzo. “I'm sure the answer to that is within this letter, sir.”

Lorenzo opened up the envelope. “I recognize the handwriting, no doubt. It’s beautiful handwriting. And as white as the paper this writing is on, the beautiful hand that wrote it is whiter.”

“I believe it’s a love letter,” said Gratiano, while he observed his friend absorbed in reading it.

After a second, Launcelot became impatient. He had much to do today for his new master's feast. “May I go, sir?” he asked.

“Where are you going?” Lorenzo asked.

“Sir, I have to go invite my old master the Jew to join tonight with my new master the Christian.”

Lorenzo found a piece of paper and quickly scribbled out a note. “Hold on, take this: tell gentle Jessica I will not fail her. Tell her privately.” He handed the note to Launcelot, who promptly left. “Go on, gentlemen. Get ready for the masquerade tonight. I have someone who can be a torch-bearer.”

“Okay, I’ll go ahead and get right on it,” Salanio said.

“So will I,” said Salarino.

“Meet me and Gratiano at Gratiano’s house in an hour,” said Lorenzo, as the two men left.

“Wasn’t that letter from Jessica?” asked Gratiano. He couldn't help not knowing.

“I have to tell you everything. She has told me how I can get her out of her father’s house and what gold and jewels she has. She described a page’s suit she has ready. If the Jew her father ever makes it to heaven, it will be because of her. She’ll never suffer from bad luck unless it happens because of one reason: that she is the daughter of an unbelieving Jew. Come on, go with me. Read this as we go.” Lorenzo handed Gratiano the note. “Beautiful Jessica is going to be my torch-bearer.”

Chapter 5

"Well, you'll see how it is—you'll see it with your own eyes, the difference between working for old Shylock and Bassanio," said Shylock in a loud voice as he paced in his house. Launcelot's resignation had come as a complete surprise to him. To know that he was losing his servant to his own money was an insult as well. Launcelot clutched his hat in his hands as he received the reprimand. "Jessica!—you will not eat so greedily as you have done here—Jessica!— and sleep and snore, and wear your cloths out— Jessica, come here, I'm calling you!"

"Jessica!" Launcelot joined in, hoping to get this confrontation over as quickly as possible.

"Why do you call her? I didn't tell you to call her."

"You always told me I couldn't do anything unless you said I could."

Jessica walked into the living room. "Did you call? What do you want?"

"I am invited for dinner, Jessica, so here are my keys." Shylock handed her the ring of keys. "But why should I go? The invite is not because they like me. They're just flattering me. But I'll go out of spite, to feast at the expense of the wasteful Christian. Jessica, my girl, look after the house. I am hesitant to go. There's something up that is making me uneasy. I know because I dreamt of money bags last night."

"Please, sir, go. My new master is expecting you to approach," pleaded Launcelot.

"And I expect his reproach."

"And they have been making plans. I will not say you will see a masquerade, but if you do, then it wasn't for nothing that my nose started bleeding on this past Easter Monday at six o'clock in the morning, exactly like it did on Ash Wednesday four years ago in the afternoon."

"What, there's going to be a masquerade? Listen to me, Jessica, lock up my doors and when you hear the drum and the disgusting squealing of the crooked flute don't crawl up to the windows or stick your head out to look into the street to look at the Christian fools with painted faces. Instead, plug up my house's ears, I mean my windows. Don't let the sound of shallow foolishness enter my serious house. By Jacob's staff, I swear, I'm not in the mood to go out feasting tonight, but I will go. Go on ahead of me, then, And tell them I will come."

“I will go ahead, sir.” Shylock waved Launcelot away and paced out of the room. Launcelot moved closer to Jessica and began to whisper. “Mistress, look out the window later, and you will see the arrival of a Christian boy well worth the glance of a Jewess’ eye.” He did not even wait for her acknowledgment as he sprung out of the room.

“What did that fool say to you, huh?” Shylock spotted the boy right before he left.

“He said ‘Goodbye mistress,’ and nothing else,” responded Jessica.

“The fool is nice enough, but he eats a lot. He is slow as a snail when he works, and he naps as much as a cat. Bees that don’t work can’t stay in my hive so I am letting him go, and letting him work for the one that will have help to waste the money he borrowed from me. Well, Jessica, go inside. I may very well return immediately. Do as I tell you and shut the doors behind you. Lock things up and you will find them where you left them, which is a saying that is always fresh in a thrifty mind.” He grabbed the coat from beside the door and left.

Jessica closed and locked the door behind him. “Goodbye, and if my luck holds out, I will lose a father and you will lose a daughter.”

Chapter 6

Gratiano and Salarino waited in the street, dressed up and in masques.

“This is the roof that Lorenzo wants us to wait under,” Gratiano paced.

“It’s after the time he said he’d be here.”

“It is surprising that he is late because lovers are usually early.”

“Yes, time flies ten times faster for those who are newly in love than it does for those who have been married a long time and are trying to remain faithful!”

"That's the case for a lot of things. Who rises from a feast with the same sharp appetite as when he sat down? Where is a horse that can retrace again his careful footsteps with the same intense heat with which he first ran them? All the things we want are chased after with more enthusiasm than they are enjoyed. Just like a fashionable young man or a favorite son—a fully decked out ship leaves her bay, lovingly embraced by the wind, but like the prodigal son she returns, with weather worn ribs and ragged sails, made lean, torn and destitute by the same wind."

"Here comes Lorenzo. We can talk more about this later."

Lorenzo approached the pair from down the street. "My good friends, thanks for your patience with my delay. It wasn't me, but my business, that made me late. When you, too, have to be thieves to get your wives, I'll wait as long for you, then. Come here," Lorenzo led them down some streets until they reached a house in the ghetto section. "This is the house of my future father-in-law. Hello!" Lorenzo yelled up at a window. "Who's inside?"

The tall window opened to reveal Jessica, dressed up in boys' clothes. She leaned out and spotted Lorenzo. "Who are you? Tell me, so I can be certain, although I swear I know you by your voice."

"It's Lorenzo, your love," he answered.

“Lorenzo, for certain, and my love for sure. Who else do I love so much? Who knows now but you, Lorenzo, whether I am yours?”

“As God is my witness, you know you are mine.”

Jessica smiled and reached down to pick something up. She leaned out again and held in her hand a small box. “Here, catch this box—it will be worth the trouble.” She dropped it to Lorenzo, who caught it. “I am glad it is dark and you can not see me because I am ashamed of my appearance. But love is blind and lovers cannot see the silly things they do. If they could, Cupid himself would blush to see me transformed into a boy.”

“Come down because you are to be my torchbearer.”

“Really, I have to hold a light to my disgrace? My disguise is, in fact, itself a bit sleazy. The light will serve to reveal what really should be kept hidden.”

“You are still sweet even when you are dressed like a boy. Come on, let’s hurry—

The night is passing and we are late for Bassanio’s feast.”

“I will lock the doors and grab some more money and be right down.” She closed the shutters and disappeared behind them.

“I think she acts more a Gentile than a Jew,” said Gratiano.

“Damn, but I love her like crazy! She is wise, if I’m observing correctly, and beautiful, if my eyes see right. And she is loyal, and has proven that. And with her being so wise, beautiful and faithful, She will have a place in my heart forever.” Jessica opened the door to her house and came out into the street. “Well, you’ve finally come down? Let’s go, gentlemen! Our mascarading friends are waiting for us.”

Lorenzo, Jessica, and Salarino walked happily along. Gratiano walked a little behind, watching his friends and wondering of where this new love would take him. After a little while, the sound of jogging footsteps called his attention behind him.

It was Antonio, who caught with Gratiano. “Signior Antonio!” said Gratiano.

“Gratiano! Where is everybody? It’s nine o’clock—our friends are waiting for you. There won’t be a masquerade tonight. The wind has turned direction, and Bassianio wants to ship out tonight. I’ve got twenty men out looking for you.”

“I’m glad to hear it. I can’t think of anything more I’d rather do than to leave tonight.”

Chapter 7

One of the rooms in Portia's house was rarely used. It stood off to the side of the main structure, having been constructed only a few years ago, and was only connected to the house through the wall, with those wishing to enter having to exit the house proper to reach it. While the room had a wonderful view of the garden, it was almost entirely unfurnished, save for a curtain that arced in front of the wall from the entrance.

This night was different though and the mostly unused room was shook with the sounds of trumpets. The door was opened to let Portia and the Prince of Morocco in. Portia's servants arranged themselves throughtout the room.

Once everyone had found their place, Portia spoke up. “Open the curtains to reveal the trunks to this noble prince.” The servants obliged and pulled the ropes that revealed three stands upon which stood a box each. “Now, make your choice.”

While Portia's attendants had seen this all play out before, the Moroccan's hadn't. They peeked over each other's shoulders and made a rabble. To appease them, the prince started to describe what he saw.

“The first box is made of gold and it bear this inscription: ‘Whoever chooses me will get what many men want.’ The second, which is made of silver, bears the promise: ‘Whoever chooses me will get all that he deserves.’ The third, made of dull lead, bears a blunt warning: ‘Whoever chooses me must give and risk all he has.’ How can I know which one to choose?”

“One of them contains my picture, prince. If you choose that one, then I am yours forever, and so is the picture.”

“I need a god to help me decide! Let me see— I will take a look at the inscriptions again. What’s it say on this lead trunk? ‘Whoever chooses me must give and risk all he has.’ Must give all, for what? Lead? Risk all for lead? This trunk seems threatening. Men that risk all do it in hope of much gain. A golden mind will not stoop to pick up things that look like garbage. I’ll then give nothing or risk anything for lead. What does the silver one that is shining like new say? ‘Whoever chooses me will get all that he deserves.’ As much as he deserves! Stop for a moment and think, Moroccan, and weigh your worth fairly. If you have a good reputation, you deserve enough, but enough might not be enough to include this lady. And yet to be afraid of my own worthiness would be to underestimate myself. As much as I deserve! Well, I deserve the lady. By birthright I deserve her, and by my wealth, by my talents and my fine upbringing and even more than all of these, by my love I deserve her.”

The prince paused for a moment and stared at the boxes quietly. The tension in the room build. "What if I didn't consider any further and stopped right here? Let's look one more time at what the inscription on the gold one says: 'Whoever chooses me will get want many men want.' Why, that's Portia. Every man in the world desires her. From all around the world they come to court her, to kiss this shrine and see this living and breathing saint. Through the Hyrcanian deserts and the vast wilds of Arabia with frequency princes travel just to lay eyes on her. The ocean, with its deep waters and high waves that lift to the sky do not present a barrier to stop the foreigners—they still come as if simply crossing a brook to see beautiful Portia. One of these three trunks contains her beautiful picture. Is it the lead trunk that contains her picture? It would be a sin to even think such a low thought. It would be too gross to put her image in that grave-like trunk. Should I think her picture is closed inside the silver trunk, being ten times less in value than the gold? Oh, that's a sinful thought! A rich gem such as she should never be placed in anything less than gold. In England they have a coin that bears the likeness of an angel stamped in gold, that's a carving. In this case, an angel in a golden bed lies inside. Give me the key: I make my choice, and will see what happens!"

An attendant behind Portia held in his hands a ring with three keys, each matching one of the boxes. He unhooked the gold one and handed it to Portia. "Here, take the key, prince," she said, "and if my picture is inside, then I am yours."

The prince took the key and opened the gold box. Under its lid there laid a skull. "Damn! What is this? A skull. And placed in its empty eye is a piece of paper with writing on it." He reached inside, took the small scroll, and unfurled it. "All that glitters is not gold, you've heard that said often. Many men have sold their souls just to find a golden surface. Graves with gold headstones hold worms. If you have been as wise as you were bold, with an old man's wisdom despite your youth, you wouldn't be reading this now. Farewell—you made the wrong guess. Wrong, for sure, and your work is for nothing. So, goodbye, desire, and welcome, hopelessness!" The prince quietly laid the piece of paper back into the box, then turned to Portia. "Portia, goodbye. My heart is too sad to stay any longer. As a loser, I'm leaving."

The prince left the room and headed out of the Belmont estate entirely. His every attendant followed him.

"Good riddance," said Portia. "Draw the curtains and leave. I hope everyone dark like him chooses the same way."

Chapter 8

Salarino and Salanio were still dressed up, but no longer wore there masques. With their dinner having been canceled, they were now wandering Venice quietly wondering where they could get a good meal this late at night.

"Well, I saw Bassanio sail away and Gratiano went along with him," remembered Salarino.
"I'm sure Lorenzo is not on their ship."

"That lowlife Jew complained to the duke, who went with him to search Bassanio's ship," said Salanio.

"He was too late—the ship was already under sail. When he got there, the duke heard someone say that a gondola had been spotted with Lorenzo and his lover Jessica in it. Besides that, Antonio assured the duke that Lorenzo and Jessica were not on Bassanio's ship."

“I’ve never heard such a confused outburst— so startling, unexpected and all over the place as the way the dog Jew cried out in the streets. ‘My daughter! My ducats! My daughter! Ran away with a Christian! My Christian ducats! Justice! The law! My ducats and my daughter! A sealed bag, two sealed bags of ducats, Of double ducats, stolen from me by my daughter! And jewels, two jewels, two rich and precious jewels, Stolen by my daughter! Justice! Find the girl. She has my jewels and the ducats.’”

“All the boys in Venice are following him, Crying ‘his stones, his daughter and his ducats.’”

“Antonio had better be sure to pay the loan on time, or he will pay for this.”

“Yes, that’s a good thing to remember. I was talking with a Frenchman yesterday who told me that in the narrow sea between France and England, there was a wreck of a ship from our country full of treasure. I thought about Antonio when I heard this and silently prayed it was not his ship.”

“You should probably tell Antonio what you heard, but do it gently so as not to upset him.”

“There’s not a kinder man on this earth. I saw Bassanio and Antonio saying goodbye: Bassanio told him he would hurry back and Antonio answered, ‘Don’t rush your business for my sake, Bassanio, but stay as long as you need to stay. As for the loan that I owe the Jew— don’t even think about it. Be happy and put your mind to wooing your love and the displays of love as will help you to win her while you are there.’ And then, with tears in his eyes, he looked away, but he offered his hand and with extraordinary affection he shook Bassanio’s hand and they parted.”

“I think he only loves the world because of Bassanio. How about we go and find him and try to lift his sadness and find a way to cheer him up?”

“Let’s do that,” agreed Salarino. And if there was food to be found at Antonio's, there would be no objections.

Chapter 9

The room with the three boxes was in use again. Nerissa and a servant were bustling around inside it, making things presentable.

"Hurry, hurry—draw the curtains right away!" said Nerissa. "The Prince of Arragon has sworn in, and he's coming to make his choice soon."

The trumpets sounded and again, Portia entered with her attendants. The Arragonian prince and his entourage followed afterward. "Look there," said Portia as she pointed to three boxes. "Those are the trunks, noble prince. If you choose the one with my picture in it, we will be married right away. But if you fail, you must not say anything more, and must leave from here immediately."

"I am under oath to do three things," said the prince. The swearing in was brisk and he wanted to clarify the terms. "First, I must never tell anyone which trunk it was that I chose. Next, if I fail to pick the right trunk I must never in my life ask a woman to marry me. And last, if I don't make the right choice I must leave immediately."

“Everyone has to swear to the same orders who come to take a chance to win me as a prize.”

“And now I’m ready. May good luck reward my heart’s hope! Gold, silver and lead. ‘Whoever chooses me must give and risk all that he has.’ You’d have to be more beautiful for me to give it all or risk it. Let’s see what the golden trunk says. Well! Let me see: ‘Whoever chooses me will get what many men want.’ What many men want! By ‘many men’ it means the foolish masses who chose by what looks good, and not by figuring out what is there beyond the looks. That kind of thinking doesn’t look at what’s inside, but—like a martin—builds its nests exposed on the outside walls despite possible violence and destruction. I will not choose what many men want because I will not jump on the bandwagon and go along with what the uncivilized masses want.” The prince turned to the people in the room for approval, but only received it from his. Portia and her attendants stood by, staring sternly at him to make his decision.

“Well, I’m guessing it is the silver trunk. Let see again what its inscription says. ‘Whoever chooses me will get all that he deserves.’ That’s well said, for who would expect to gain riches and be upright without deserving it? No one should assume they should get what they don’t deserve. If high rank, degrees and offices were not gained by corruption, but earned with honer by the person who gains them, how many men would have a position that now do not! How many would be commanded that now command! How many upper ranks would be shown to be peasants if rank were based on good name. And how many dignified would be picked from the discarded who’ve been tossed aside to become newly decked out! Well, anyway—regarding my choice: ‘Whoever chooses me will get all that he deserves.’ I will assume I am deserving. Give me the key for this trunk and I will unlock it to find my fate.”

Portia handed him the silver key. He took it and unlocked the casket. The prince opened the lid and stared into the box. He did not react nor say a word to what he saw inside for some seconds, and the room's anticipation grew.

“You’re taking to long to say what it is you found in there,” said Portia. It had only been ten seconds or so, but those seconds seem much longer when nothing is happening in a room full of people.

The prince remained silent still for a few more seconds, then turned up with his face red. "What's this? A picture of a blind idiot showing me a list! I will read it. This picture looks nothing like Portia! This is not what I'd hoped for and it is not what I deserve! 'Whoever chooses me will get all that he deserves.' Do I not deserve more that a picture of an idiot? Is this my prize? Do I deserve no better?"

"Finding offense and judging what you deserve come from places completely opposite in feeling."

"What is this?" The prince asked again as he picked up the list. He began to read it out loud. "This trunk has gone through fire seven times. Seven times to make sure the person who chooses it did not choose it wrongly. Some will kiss shadows and those will have only the happiness shadow's can bring. There are fools alive on this earth, I know, who are silver haired the same way as this trunk. Take whatever wife you will, but you will always have a fool's head like the one in the picture. So, go away —your work was quick here." He placed the list back into the box. "I will appear more the fool the longer I stay. I came here with a fool's head, but I leave with two. Goodbye, I will keep my oath and will calmly endure my misfortune."

The prince exited the estate with his attendants, leaving Portia and Belmont behind.

“They were singed like moths to the candle!” said Portia. “Oh, those calculating fools! When they choose, they have just about enough wisdom to lose.”

“The ancient saying is no lie: men die and marry by destiny,” added Nerissa.

“Please, close the curtain, Nerissa.”

A servant came into the small room. “Madam, there is at your gate a young Venetian who is coming ahead to announce the arrival of his lord. He delivers very polite greetings and—besides the courteous words— he brings gifts of great value. I have not seen such a promising suitor so far. A day in April could not be so sweet to show the promise of summer to come as this messenger shows of his lord.”

“Please, say nothing else,” said Portia. I am almost afraid you will say he is somehow related to you. You put so much energy into praising him. Let’s go, Nerissa, I want to see this potential love who has been so well announced.”

“Lord, I so hope it is Bassanio!” added Nerissa to herself.

Part Three

Chapter 1

Salanio met up with Salarino.

"Now what's the news on the Rialto?" Salanio asked his friend.

Salarino shook his head sadly. "There's a rumor that Antonio had a ship full of treasure wrecked in the English Channel. On the place called the Goodwins, I think, a very dangerous flat that proves fatal to ships. Many tall ships have sunk there, if the rumors I hear are correct."

"I wish the rumors were not true, in the way that a bitter widow tried to make her neighbors believe she cried for the death of her third husband. But it is true, without any wordiness or going on about the matter—the good Antonio, the honest Antonio—Oh, I just wish I had a title worthy enough to say how he is!"

"C'mon, what's the story?"

"What are you saying? The point is, he has lost a ship."

"I would hope that is all he loses."

“Let me say ‘amen’ at once unless the devil should cross the path of my prayer, for here comes the devil looking like a Jew.” Salanio spotted Shylock, who approached them. “Hey there, Shylock What’s the news among the merchants?”

“You knew—nobody knew as well as you—about my daughter’s plans to flee.” Shylock spoke in a raised voice.

“That’s true,” said Salarino, with an expression of mock guilt. “I, myself, knew the tailor who made the wings she flew away on.”

“And Shylock, for his part, knew she was ready to run away—she had that look about her of any child that is about to leave the home,” added Salanio.

“She is damned for it,” said Shylock.

“That would be for certain, if it’s the devil judging her.”

“My own flesh and blood turned against me!”

“Really? Your flesh turns against you at its age?”

“I mean my daughter is my flesh and blood.”

"There is more difference between your flesh and hers than between black and white," began Salarino. "And more difference between your blood than there is between red wine and white wine. But tell us—have you heard whether Antonio has had any loss at sea or not?"

"That's another bad bargain—a bankrupt, a squanderer, who can hardly show his head on the Rialto. A beggar who used to look so smug at the market. Let him think about his loan. He was so ready to call me on my excessive interest. Let him think about his loan. He was willing to lend money interest free, but now let him think about his own loan."

"Well, to be sure, if he forfeits it you won't take his flesh—what good would it be?"

"I'll use it to bait fish. If it will feed nothing else it will feed my revenge. He disgraces me and cost me a half million. He laughed at my losses, mocked my gains, scorned my nation, defeated my bargains, caused my friends to turn against me, angered my enemies, and for what? I am a Jew: that's why. Doesn't a Jew have eyes? Doesn't a Jew have hands, organs, size, senses, feelings and emotions? We eat the same food, are wounded by the same weapons, susceptible to the same diseases, healed by the same methods, warmed and cooled by the same winter and summer, just like a Christian is? If you prick us, don't we bleed? If you tickle us, don't we laugh? If you poison us, don't we die? And if you wrong us, won't we seek revenge? If we are like you in every other way, we will be like you in that way, too. If a Jew wronged a Christian what is his punishment? Revenge. If a Christian wrongs a Jew, what should his suffering be by the example of the Christian? Yes, revenge. The discourtesy you teach me, I will carry out, and I will do it more extremely than the way I learned it."

A young approached Salarino and Salanio. "Sirs, my master Antonio is at his house and he would like to speak to both of you."

"We've been looking all over for him," said Salarino, eager for the chance to leave. They were thankfully aided by the arrival of Tubal.

“Here comes another Jew,” said Salanio. “A third could do match these first two, unless the devil himself turned Jewish.” Salanio and Salarino left with the manservant, leaving Shylock to speak with Tubal.

“Hello, Tubal! What’s the news from Genoa? Have you found my daughter?”

“I’ve heard talk about her in all the places I’ve been, but I haven’t found her.”

“What, this is too much! A diamond gone that cost me two thousand ducats in Frankfort! The curse of being of Jew is something I have never felt until now. Two thousand ducats lost in that diamond, and other precious, precious jewels. I wish my daughter were dead at my feet with the jewels in her ears! I wish she were in a coffin at my feet, and the ducats were in the coffin with her! No news of them? I do not even know what I’m spending trying to find them. Loss after loss! The thief got away with so much, and it’s taking so much to find the thief. And there’s no satisfaction, no revenge. I’ve had no luck except the bad luck I’m having right now. No one is complaining about it but me. No one is crying except for my own tears.”

“Well, other men are having bad luck, too. Antonio, as I heard in Genoa-”

"What? What? Bad luck? Bad luck?"

"His ship coming from Tripolis wrecked."

"Oh, thank God! Thank God! Is it true? Is it true?"

"I spoke with some of the sailors that survived the wreck."

"Thank you, Tubal! That's good news! Good news! Ha ha! Where did you hear that? In Genoa?"

"Your daughter spent a lot of money in Genoa. I heard in one night she spent eighty ducats."

"Oh, you stick a knife in me! I will never see my gold again—eighty ducats in one night! Eighty ducats!"

"Several of Antonio's creditors who I traveled with to Venice swear that he has no choice but to break his promise to pay you."

"I am glad to know this. I will torment and torture him about it. I am glad to know this."

"One of the creditors showed me a ring he had of yours that your daughter had given him to pay for a monkey."

"I am so angry with her! That tortured me, Tubal—that was my turquoise ring. Leah gave it to me before we were married. I would not have given it up for a jungle full of monkeys."

"Antonio is certainly ruined."

"That's true, very true. Go, Tubal, and pay a police officer to arrest Antonio. Speak with him two weeks ahead of time. I will have the heart of Antonio if he forfeits. If he was not in Venice, I can make whatever deals I want. Go, go, Tubal, and meet me at our synagogue. Go, good Tubal. I'll see you there, Tubal."

Chapter *2*

Upon arriving at Belmont, Bassanio and Portia hit it off, remembering the enjoyable time they had when he had visited long ago. They walked and laughed, while Gratiano, Nerissa and attendants followed a few steps behind, happy to see that for once, Portia enjoyed the company of a suitor.

“I beg you, please wait a day or two before you make your guess,” said Portia. “If you choose wrong I will lose your company. So, wait awhile. There’s something tells me, but it’s not love, that I will not lose you, and you know yourself that I would not feel that way if I hated you. But just in case you don’t understand me well— and because girls aren’t really supposed to say what’s on our minds I would like for you to stay here a month or two before you take a chance to win me. I could tell you how to choose correctly, but I am sworn not to, so I won’t do that. So, you might lose me. But if you do, you’ll make me wish I’d done the wrong thing— that I had told you even though I swore I will not. Your eyes tempt me. They have looked me over and have divided me. One half of me is yours and the other half is yours, too— The half that should be mine, but if it’s mine, then it’s yours, So it is all yours. But these awful times put obstacles between the owners and their claim! And so, even so I am yours, I am not yours. If this proves to be the case then it is because luck has gone bad, not because of me. I’m talking too much. It’s just to prolong time, to stretch it out and draw it out and to keep you from making your choice.”

“Let me choose.” said Bassanio. “Not knowing like this is torturing me.”

“Punished for your crime, Bassanio! Then do confess: what betrayal is mixed in with your love.”

"Simply the ugly betrayal of not being able to trust I will even be able to enjoy you as my love. There is as much relation between snow and fire as there is between betrayal and my love for you."

"Ah, but I'm afraid you might be speaking like one who is being punished who will say anything under the stress."

"Promise you will let me live and I'll confess the truth."

"Well, in that case, confess and live."

" 'Confess' and 'love' are what my confession amounts to. Oh, what happy torture, when my tormenter tells me the answers that set me free! But please let me take my chances with the trunks."

"Well, let's go then!" Portia led the group to the small room. She explained to him the premise of the deal and added "I am locked inside one of them. If you love me, you will figure out which one. Nerissa and everybody else, stand back from him." Everyrone followed Portia's request, giving Bassanio enough room that their own talking wouldn't bother him.

“Let music play while he makes his choice. Then, if he loses, he will find his swan-song in the music. To make it even more so and proper like a swan-song, my eyes will cry the tears to make a stream which will be the watery death bed of the swan. But he might win. What music should we play in that case? That music should be like the fanfare that loyal subjects bow to when a king is newly crowned. Just like the sweet music that plays at daybreak that a drowsy bridegroom hears when he wakes on his wedding day. Bassanio is walking toward the trunks with no less dignity but with much more love than the young Hercules when he freed the virgin princess sacrificed at Troy from the sea monster. I'll be like the princess and everyone else can be like wives at Troy, crrying as we look on and watch to see the result of the challenge. Go, Hercules! If you live, I live. I feel much, much more distress watching the struggle than you feel in making it.”

As Bassanio looked over the caskets, one of the attendants had brought back her lute and began singing. “Tell me where is love born, In the heart or in the head? How is it started and how is it fed? Answer. Answer. It starts in the eyes, and is fed with gazes, and love dies Wwhen it is still just an infant. Let us all ring bells to mourn love's passing I'll start—Ding, dong, bell.”

“What shows on the outside does not reveal what is inside,” Bassanio thought to himself as the music played. “The world is often deceived with pretty attire. In the court, people can plead not guilty when they are tainted and corrupt, and if they do in a pleasing voice may cover any signs of guilt. In religion, some men can defend a sinful act by putting on a serious face and make it seem good by reading from the Bible, and in that way hide the sin with pretty words. There is no common sin that can’t be made to take on the appearance of seeming good by changing how it looks. How many cowards, whose courage is about as strong as a staircase made of sand, wear on their chins beards like Hercules or Mars, the god of war, even though if you look inside you will find them fearful? But they wear these beards as signs of strength to try to make people afraid of them! Look at beauty, too— and you will see it can be acquired with lots of makeup, which works miracles on natural looks, making those that wear it most seem promiscious. It’s the same thing with curly, blond hair— which blows so playfully and spirited in the wind, and is supposed to make a woman seem more beautiful, but it is often a wig made from the head of a woman whose skull is in the grave. So outward beauty is but a golden shore leading to a dangerous sea, like a beautiful scarf can hide a dark woman. Plainly put— what seems to be true is often a cunning disguise to trap even the wisest. So because of this, you brilliant gold— unpleasant food for Midas to eat—I won’t choose. And not the pale silver, either, which serves as a slave as coins for men to do business. But you, lead, that is of no real value and which looks more threatening than promising, and which moves me beyond eloquence— it is the one I choose. I hope I'm happy with the outcome."

"All my other feelings are flying to the air," though Portia, "doubtful thoughts and quickly embraced sadness, and fear that left me shaking and awful jealousy—they all leave! Oh, I feel love and I need to take things slowly and quiet my happiness, I need to contain my joy and try not to feel so much. I'm feeling too much happiness. I need to feel less because I am afraid I feel too much."

Noticing the servant with the keys, Bassanio didn't ask for one, but merely stepped up and politely took the key ring. He paused in front of the boxes again, then approached the lead one.

“Beautiful Portia’s picture!” He said when he opened the box. A quiet gasp rose up from Portia's attendants. “What God-like artist made this picture that looks so much like her? Are the eyes moving or do they just seem to be moving when I move my eyes? Look are her open lips parted with sweet breath—so sweet a way to part such sweet lips. Here in her hair the painter played like a spider and wove a golden mesh that can entrap the hearts of men faster than small flies in cobwebs. But her eyes— how could he keep looking to paint them? After he painted the first, it seems it would have the power to make him stop seeing and unable to paint the second one. But look, how much the subject of the picture I praise outdoes its shadow and makes it seem small, and the picture is nowhere as beautiful as its subject. Here’s a paper that contains the summary of my fortune.”

Bassanio picked up the paperand read it aloud. “You who has chosen not by looks have had good luck and made the right choice! Since this good fortune falls to you, be happy and seek nothing else. If you are happy with this and accept this fortune for your state of being, turn toward where your lady is and claim her as yours with a loving kiss. A nice note. Fair lady, with your permission, this note tells me to give you a kiss and to receive you. But like someone struggling in a contest, that things he has done well in people’s eyes, draws applause and shouting— I am still excited and energized, but wondering and not sure whether this praise is mine or not. So, wonderfully beautiful lady, I’m standing here doubting if what I see is true until it is confirmed, signed and made official by you.”

"You see me, Lord Bassanio, as I stand here, and I am what I am, though I alone wouldn't wish to be better for myself, I wish I could be better for you. I would be twenty times what I am—a thousand times more beautiful and ten thousand times richer so that you might value me more. My talents, beauties, possessions and friends, would be more than you could want. However, the full worth of me is something that amounts to the total of an unlearned girl—uneducated and innocent— and happy that she is not too old that she can learn new things, and even happier that she was not raised without the ability to be capable of learning, and happiest of all that her spirit commits itself to you to be taught. By her lord, her governor, her king: myself and all that is mine is now to you transferred. Until now I was the lord of this beautiful mansion. I was master of my servants, and Queen of myself. But even as we speak this house, these servants and even me are yours, my lord. I give them to you with this ring. If you ever part with it, lose it or give it away, it means our love is over, and I'll have the right to be angry with you."

“Madam, you’ve left me speechless. My blood is pounding in my veins in response to you. I feel so confused right now about everything, like after there is a wonderful speech made by a prince you admire, and among the crowd is applause and cheers. Everything—all blending together— becomes nothing but wild joy both shouted and not shouted about. If this ring ever leaves my finger, you can be sure I am dead. You can declare with certainty, ‘Bassanio’s dead!’”

A cheer went up. Nerissa approached the couple. “My lord and my lady, it is now time for us who have been watching this to make our wishes known and to say, Best wishes! Best wishes, my lord and lady!”

Gratiano spoke up as well. “My lord Bassanio and my gentle lady, I wish you all the happiness you could possible want, and I am sure I can wish you no more. When you are ready to take your vows to become married, I want to ask if I may get married at the same time as you.”

“Certainly, if you can find a wife by then,” said Bassanio.

"Thank you, my lord, I have gotten one because of you. I fall in love as quickly as you do—at first sight. Just as when you fell when you saw Portia, I looked at Nerrisa and fell in love as quickly as you. We both have the same right to do so. Just as your fortune depended on the trunks, so did mine, and I got right to the matter of wooing her until I began to sweat and making more effort until my mouth was dry, from declarations of love and promises until I got a promise from this beautiful lady that we would marry dependent on fortune of winning her mistress."

"Is this true, Nerissa?" asked Portia.

"Yes, Madam, if you say it is okay," answered Nerissa.

"And do you mean what you say, Gratiano?" asked Bassanio.

"Yes, I mean it, my lord," responded Gratiano.

"Then we would be honored to include you in our marriage feast."

Gratiano and Nerissa embraced. "Let's bet them a thousand ducats that we'll have the first son."

"What, and put it down now?" Nerissa asked.

"No, we'd never win the bet if I put it down!"

Footsteps from the main house drew everyone's attention. To Bassanio and Gratiano's surprise, Lorenzo, Jessica, and Salerio arrived, along with a fourth person.

“Lorenzo and Salerio, welcome!” said Bassanio. “I hope my new position as master of the house has enough power to bid you welcome. If it’s alright with you, I give my friends and countrymen a welcome, sweet Portia.”

“So do I, my lord. They are totally welcome.” She added.

“Thank you,” said Lorenzo. “It wasn’t my intention, my lord, to come here to see you. I met with Salerio along the way and he insisted, with no room for me to say no, that I come along with him!”

“I did that, my lord, and I have good reason. Signior Antonio sends his grettings.” Salerio handed Bassanio an envelope.

“Before I open this, please tell me how Antonio is doing,” asked Bassanio.

Salerio considered how to answer. “He’s not sick, my lord, but he is worried. He’s not well, but he is very worried. This letter will reveal what’s going on.”

Bassanio stepped out of the room to read the letter in silence. “Nerrisa, welcome this man,” said Gratiano. “Say hello to her, too, Salerio. What’s the word from Venice? How is the merchant Antonio doing? I know he will be glad to hear of our success. We are the Jasons who have won the Golden Fleece.”

“I wish you had won what he has lost.”

“Whatever is written in that letter is hard news.” Portia looked at Bassanio. “It is making Bassanio turn pale to read it. Some dear friend must have died—I can’t think of anything else in the world that would change the mood of a stable man so much. Look! He seems worse and worse!” She spoke up to grab her fiance's attention. “With your permission, Bassanio: I am your other half, So let me bear half of whatever it is this letter brings to you.”

Bassanio briskly walked back to the group. "Oh sweet Portia, What is here are the most unpleasant words that ever stained paper! Kind lady, when I first told you I love you. I told you that all the wealth I have runs in my vein—that I was born noble, and then I told you the truth, but still, dear lady, when I said I have nothing, you will see that I was bragging. When I said I had nothing, I should have told you, as well, that I have worse than nothing, for, it's true, I asked a favor of a dear friend and he borrowed money from his enemy to help me out. In this letter, lady, the paper seems like the body of my friend. With every word like a huge wound bleeding all over the place. Is it true, Salerio, have all his ships at sea failed? Did not one survive? From Tripolos and Mexico and England, from Lisbon, Barbary and India? Not one of the ships escaped being wrecked on merchant-ruining rocks?"

"Not one, my lord," said Salerio with heavy sigh. "Besides, it looks as though even if he had the money to pay off the Jew, the Jew would not take it. Never have I known a creature that looked so much like a man so ready and eager to ruin a man. He's at the duke both morning and night saying the freedom of the state will be harmed if they deny him justice. Twenty merchants, the duke himself, and the Venetian leaders of highest standing have all tried to convince him, but no one can convince his not to go after the claim written in the loan papers regarding non-payment."

Jessica spoked up. “When I was with my father I heard him swear to Tubal and to Chus, fellow Jews, that he would rather have Antonio’s flesh than twenty times the value of the loaned amount that Antonio owed him. And I know, my lord. that is the law, authory and power can not stop it, It will be hard for poor Antonio.”

“Is it your dear friend who is in this trouble?” asked Portia.

“He is my dearest friend and the kindest man,” affirmed Bassanio. “He had the best disposition and a great spirit and has the best manners. He is the sort of man the ancient Roman idea of honor appears in more than any other man in Italy.”

“How much does he owe the Jew?

“He owes him three thousand ducats.”

"What, that's all? Pay him six thousand and be done with the debt. Double the six thousand, and then triple it before this great friend as you've described him loses a hair through your fault. But first, let's go to church and get married. And then you should go to Venice to be with your friend. You would never sleep by my side otherwise without a restless soul. You will have enough gold to pay this petty debt twenty times over. When it is paid, bring your friend back here. Nerissa and I, in the meantime will live like virgins and widows. Let's go! You will leave once you are married. Welcome your friends and put on a happy face. Since it is costing so much to have you, I will love you all the more. But first, read me the letter from your friend."

Bassanio opened the letter again and read. "Sweet Bassanio, my ships have all been wrecked, my creditors are growing cruel, my wealth is very low, my loan to the Jew is forfeited, and since I'm not paying it, it is impossible to live, all debts between you and I are cleared if I could just see you when I die. I understand that if you don't want to come because of your affection for me this letter will not convince you to do so."

"Oh, my love—take care of things and go on!"

"Since I have your blessing in going away, I will hurry back. But, until I return, know that I will not sleep in any bed. I will not rest until I am with you again."

Chapter 3

"Jailer, keep an eye on this one." Shylock pointed at Antonio. The jailer merely nodded. "Don't try to convice me of mercy. This is the fool that lent out money without interest. Jailer, keep an eye on him."

"Listen to me, Shylock," began Antonio.

"I'll have my payment. Don't try to talk me out of getting it. I have sworn an oath the I will get my payment. You called me a dog when you had no reason to do so. So, since I am a dog, beware of my fangs. The duke will give me justice. I do wonder, however, why this jailer is so bad, to allow Antonio to come out of his cell by simply asking."

"Please, listen to what I have to say."

"I will have my payment. I will not listen to you. I will have my payment. So just stop talking. I'll not be made to look like a weak and easily deceived fool to just shake my head, give up to you with a sigh and yield to Christian prayers. Don't follow me. I won't listen to you. I will have my payment."

Shylock walked away quickly, leaving Antonio standing in the streets of Venice with only the jailer and Salarino.

“He is the most impossible dog who ever lived among men,” said Salarino.

“Leave him alone,” said Antonio. “I won’t follow him anymore with my useless prayers. He wants me dead. I know his reason: I’ve given money to the people who couldn’t pay him back many times, once they’ve asked me to do so. He hates me for that reason.”

“I am sure the duke will never allow this payment for forfeit to be enforced.”

“The duke cannot deny the law. The business that strangers bring to merchants in Venice can not be denied or it would cause harm to the justice of the state since the profit of the city depends on the trade of foreigners. So, go on— these worries have caused me to lose so much weight I will hardly be able to spare a pound of flesh tomorrow to my bloody creditor. So, jailer, go away. I just hope to God Bassanio comes to see me pay his debt, and I don’t care about anything else!”

Chapter 4

"Madam," Lorenzo said to Portia, "I'd like to say in your presence that you have a noble and true understanding of real friendship, which you have shown by letting your lord go off like this. The man you are sending him to loves your lord greatly and is faithful to him. I know you might be prouder of doing what comes natural to you if you knew this."

"I've never been sorry for doing good and I won't be now," she replied. "Friends that talk and spend time together have souls that bear an equal amount of love. They must be very much alike, and have the same sort of characteristics, manners and energy. This makes me think that this Antonio, being such a close friend of my lord, must be very much like my lord. So, if that's the case, the money I've sent with him is a small amount to free the one who is like my lover out of a hellish state! But, I'm coming too close to praising myself, so let's talk of this no more. Let's talk about other things. Lorenzo, I'd like for you to take over the care and management of my house until my lord comes back. As for me — I have made a secret vow to heaven to live in prayer and meditation to be only accompanied my Nerissa until her husband and my lord come back. There is a monastery about two miles away. We will stay there. I hope you will not deny this request which my love and some need puts upon you."

"Madam, with all of my heart— I will do whatever you wish."

"My servants already know about this and will answer to you and Jessica in place of Lord Bassanio and me. So, goodbye, until we see each other again."

"I hope you find peace of mind and happiness!"

"I wish you all you hope for at this time," added Jessica.

"Thanks you for the wish, and I'm happy to wish the same back to you. Goodbye, Jessica. Take care," said Portia. Jessica and Lorenzo left, leaving Portia alone with Nerissa and one of her servants. "Now, Balthasar, I have found you to be ever honest and true, and I hope to find you that way, still. Take this letter, and with as much speed as possible for a man get to Padua. Put this letter into my cousin's—Dr. Bellario—hands. Take whatever papers and clothes he gives to you and bring them, please, as quickly as you can to the ferry—the public ferry— that goes to and from Venice. Don't waste time talking, just get going. I will be there before you."

"Madam, I will go as fast as possible," sad Balthasar. He took the letter and walked out.

"Come on, Nerissa, I have things in the works you don't know about yet. We'll see our husbands before they even think of us."

"Will they see us?" asked Nerissa.

“They will see us, Nerissa, but we will be dressed in a way that they will think we are what we are not. I will bet you that when we are both dressed like young men I will be the handsomer of the two and I will wear my sword with much more grace and speak like just like an adolescent boy with a squeaking voice, and my ladylike steps will become a manly stride. I’ll talk about frightening things like a fine bragging young man, and tell clever lies About how honorable ladies wanted my love, but when I wouldn’t give it to them, they fell sick and died I could do nothing about it! Then, I’ll feel sorry and wish that what I had done had not killed them. I’ll tell twenty of these little lies. And men will swear I just graduated from school a year ago. I have in my head a thousand of these sort of tricks for young men that I will use.”

“Why will we turn into men?”

“What sort of question is that! As if you were an improper interviewer! But, come on, I’ll tell you the whole plan when we are in my coach which is waiting for us at the park gate. We must hurry away. We have to make at least twenty miles today.”

Chapter 5

“Yes, it’s true,” said Launcelot. He had stayed behind at Bassanio's request and took some time to speak with Jessica. “Look—the sins of fathers are paid for by their children. So, I worried for you. I’ve always been direct with you and so I will say what is bothering me in this case: be happy, for I really think you are going to hell. There is only one hope for you, but that is a sort of illegitimate hope.”

“Tell me, what hope is that?” Jessica said.

“Well, you can hope that your father is not your father and that you are not the Jew’s daughter.”

“That would be an illegitimate hope, yes, and the sins of my mother would be upon me in that case.”

“Well, in that case, I’m afraid you will go to hell because of your father and your mother. If you do not fall into one trap—your father—you will fall into the other one—your mother. So, you are a goner either way.”

“I will be saved by my husband. He has made me a Christian.

"Well, he was wrong to do that. There were plenty of Christians before—as many as could stand to live near one another. Making more Christians will raise the price of pigs. We we all become pork-eaters, we will soon not even be able to afford a slice of bacon."

Lorenzo came upon the corner of the garden the two were talking in. "I'll tell my husband, Launcelot, what you have said. Here he comes."

"I'm going to grow jealous of you, Launcelot," said Lorenzo, "if you keep taking my wife into corners like this."

"You don't need to worry about us, Lorenzo. Launcelot and I are on the outs. He tells me frankly that I will not go to heaven because I am a Jew's daughter, and he also says you are not being a good citizen because by converting Jews to Christians, you are raising the price of pork."

"I think I can say I am a better citizen than you can by getting that black woman pregnant. The Moor is going to have your child, Launcelot."

"Well then," said Launcelot, "there's more of the Moor for a reason, but if she is less than an honest woman, she is certainly more than I took her for."

“Any fool is capable of making puns! I think the best quality of cleverness will soon be to stay silent, and talking will only be highly regarded in parrots. Go in and tell the servants to get ready for dinner.”

“That is done, sir. They are all hungry.”

“Good Lord, what a smart aleck you are! Then tell them to get dinner ready.”

“I believe the term you are looking for, sir, it ‘set the table.’”

“Will you set the table then?”

“No sir, that is not my responsibility.”

“You’re just finding reasons to be clever! Are you going to show me the entire range of you cleverness all at once? Please, just understand very plainly what I mean: Go in there and tell the servants to set the table, serve the meat and we will come in and eat it.”

“Regarding the table, sir, the food will be served on it. Regarding the meat, sir, it will be on covered plates. Regarding your dinner, sir, well just do what you feel is best and it will all work out.” Launcelot smiled at his own cleverness and left them.

“I can see that he is very good at playing with words! The fool has in his head an army of useful words, and I know many fools that are in a better position that know as many words as he does and engage in word play to deflect the subject at hand. How are you, Jessica? Tell me what you think about things— how do you like Lord Bassanio’s wife?”

“I like her more than I can say,” said Jessica. “It is right that Lord Bassanio lives in such an upright way and by having such a blessing as her in his life he will find more joy here on earth than in heaven. If on this earth with her he can not find happiness he shouldn’t even bother going to heaven. Really, if two gods were playing a game in heaven and placed a bet on two earthly women with Portia being one of them, there must have been something lost on the other, for the poor rude world does not contain her equal.”

“I am as good a husband for you as she is as a wife.”

“You should ask me about that!”

“I will later. First, let’s go to dinner.”

“No, let me say good things about you while I feel like it.”

“No, please, let’s talk about it at dinner. That way, no matter what you say, I’ll take it in with everything else and digest it.”

“Well, I’ll set you straight about it.”

Part Four

Chapter 1

Everyone in the Venetian court stood up as the duke entered with the magnificoes. Dressed in their most judicial clothing, they took their chairs in front of the court, facing the audience that sat down after they did.

“Is Antonio here?” the duke asked.

“Yes, I am here,” responded Antonio. Bassanio, Gratiano, and Salerio stood by him.

“I feel sorry for you. You’ve come to face a hard enemy, an inhuman wretch who is incapable of pity—a man who does not have the least amount of mercy.”

“I’ve been told you have gone to a lot of trouble to try to stop what he is planning to do. But since he is so stubborn and no legal means can keep me out of his reach, I will face him with patience to match his rage. I am ready to suffer this quietly as he acts out of cruelty and anger.”

“Someone go tell the Jew to come into the court.”

A bailiff waiting by the door exited and let in Shylock, who walked down the court's aisle to boos and hisses from the court.

“Move aside and make room so he can stand before me,” said the Duke. “Shylock, eveyone thinks, and I do, too, that even though you have carried on in a hateful way all the way to the end, it is thought that perhaps you’ll surprise us by showing some mercy and pity which would be even more remarkable than the obvious cruelty and that while you say you will take your penalty— which is a pound of this poor merchant’s flead—you will not only let that go, but, moved to kindness and compassion, you will forgive a portion of the principal, as you look with pity on his losses that have so recently weighed down on him— enough to drive any merchant down and that would extract feelings of sympathy from the unfeeling and stone-hard hearts of the most unyielding Turks and Tarters, who were never trained to offer tenderness or courtesy. We all expect a kind answer, Jew.”

“I have told you that I intend to do what I swear by Holy Sunday to have the penalty due for the forfeit of the loan. If you deny me that, it will endanger your city’s rights and freedoms. You want to know why I’d rather have a pound of rotting flesh instead of receiving three thousand ducats. I won’t answer that. Let’s just say it strikes my fancy—is that enough of an answer? What if my house had a rat in it and I wanted to pay ten thousand ducats to have it exterminated? Well, do you have your answer yet? Some men don’t like a roasted pig with its mouth open, and others go crazy if they see a cat. Others, when they get a whiff of the sound of bagpipes, cannot help but urinate. Our fancy, which is connected to our most powerful feelings, determines what we like or don’t like. So, for your answer: just as there is no good reason to be found why one man cannot stand a roasted pig and another a harmless and useful cat, and another, the coarse sound of a bagpipe, but who has to yield to a shameful act because he himself is offended— in the same way, I can’t give a reason, and I won’t, beyond a deep-rooted hate and a steady loathing for Antonio. So, I will follow through on my claim against him. Do you have your answer?”

“That is no answer, you heartless man, to excuse how cruel you are being,” said Bassanio.

“No one said my answers have to please you.”

“Tell me, do all men kill the things they do not love?”

"Does any man not want to kill the thing he hates?"

"Not every annoyance is hated at first."

"What, would you let a snake bite you twice?"

"Please, why are you arguing with the Jew?" Antonio asked Bassanio. "You may as well go stand on the beach and ask the largest waves to decrease in height. You may as well as the wolf why he killed a lamb and made its mother cry. You may as well tell the pines in the mountains to stop swaying and to be quiet when the wind blows and moves through them. You may as well attempt to do anything just as impossible than to try to soften his hard Jewish heart. I beg you, don't make him any more offers, and do try anything else. Let's make this brief and as easy as possible— let me have my punishment and give the Jew what he wants."

"Instead of three thousand ducats, here is six," Bassanio ignored Antonio, desperate to save him.

"If every ducat were six thousand ducats, and then six times that, I would not have them. I will have my payment."

"How can you ever hope for mercy when you give none?" the duke asked.

“What punishment should I dread, since I do no wrong? You have in your possession many slaves you’ve bought which— like your donkeys and your dogs and mules— you use to do despicable things just because they are slaves and you bought them. What if I said to you, ‘Set them free and let them marry your children,’ and ‘Why are you making them work so hard?’ or ‘Give them beds as soft as your and please their palates with the same food you eat?’ You would answer, ‘The slaves are mine.’ and so I answer you the same. I demand the pound of flesh— I paid a lot for it. It is mine and I will have it. If you deny me, your laws will mean nothing! You will not be able to enforce the rules of Venice. I’m waiting for my payment. Answer me: will I have it?”

“I will dismiss the court for the day unless Bellario, a wise expert of the law whom I sent for to help make the judgment, Shows up today.”

“Outside there waits a messenger with letters from the doctor, who is arriving from Padua,” said Salerio.

“Bring us the letters and call in the messenger,” said the duke. The bailiff went

“Cheer up, Antonio!” Bassanio said. “Keep up your courage! The Jew can have my flesh, blood, bones everything— before I let you lose one drop of blood for me.”

“I am the diseased sheep in the flock, most fit for death,” said Antonio. “The weakest of the fruit falls to the ground first. Let me be the one. I can’t think of a better purpose, Bassanio, than for you to live and write my epitaph.”

A lawyer's clerk entered the court and approached the front.

“Have you come from Padua- from Bellario’s?” asked the Duke.

“From both, sir. Bellario sends his greetings,” answered the clerk, presenting a letter to the duke proving such.

Bassanio noticed that Shylock had taken out a knife and was sharpening it. “Why are you sharpening your knife so eagerly?” he asked.

“To cut my payment from that bankrupt man over there,” Shylock responded.

“You shouldn’t do it on the sole of your shoe, but on your soul, cruel Jew,” Gratiano sid. “You’d sharpen the knife better than any metal can. Not even the hangman’s ax could be half as sharp as the hate inside you. Can no prayers reach you?”

“No, none that you have the intelligence to make.”

“Oh, go to hell, you unmovable dog! You should be killed in the name of justice. You almost cause me to be unsteady in my beliefs, and to agree with the philosopher Pythagoras that the souls of animals are born again as humans. Your dog-like soul came from a wolf who was slaughtered for killing humans. As he hung from the gallows his savage soul fled and—while you were in the unholy womb of your mother— it came into you. Your desires are wolfish, bloody, starved and insatiable.”

“Until you can rant the seal off of my contract, you just hurt your lungs to yell so loudly. Recover your senses, young man, or you will fall apart. I have the law on my side.”

The duke finished reading the letters from the clerk. “This letter from Bellario recommends a young and well-educated legal expert to our court. Where is he?”

“He waits nearby,” said the clerk, “to hear whether you will admit him into the court.”

“I welcome him with all of my heart. Three or four of you go give him a courteous escort here. In the meantime, the court will hear Bellario’s letter.” As the bailiff and some guards went to find the lawyer, the duke handed the letter back to the clerk.

The clerk began to read aloud. “Please understand that even though I received your letter, I am very ill at the time. However, when your messenger delivered the letter, I was being visited by a young doctor from Rome whose name is Balthasar. I told him about the controversy regarding the Jew and Antonio the merchant. We looked over many books together. He is aware of my opinion on the matter, which was made better with his knowledge, which is so broad I could not recommend him more, and he brings my opinion with him, since I am not able to do so, and will fill your request in place of me. Please do not let his young age fool you into thinking he is not worthy of respect and high esteem. I've never known such a young body graced with such a wise head. I leave him for you to accept into court. Once you see what he can do, he will commend himself by his actions.”

“You hear what the wise Bellario has written,” said the Duke. The bailiffs and the guards returned with a fourth person. “ And here comes the expert he recommends.” The lawyer walked up to the front. “Please, shake my hand. Have you come from Bellario?”

“I did, sir,” said the lawyer.

“Welcome, and please take a seat. Are you acquainted with the case that is currently before the court?”

“I am thoroughly familiar with the case. Which is the merchant, here, and which is the Jew?”

“Antonio and Shylock, please step forward.”

“Is your name Shylock?” the lawyer asked the Shylock.

“My name is Shylock,” he confirmed.

“The case you present is very strange, yet is so valid that the Venetian law cannot dispute it as you go forward with it.” The lawyer looked at Antonio. “You stand within danger here, don’t you?”

“Yes, that’s what he says.”

“Do you acknowledge the contract?”

“I do.”

“Then the Jew must show mercy.”

“Why should I do that?” Shylock said with a scoff. “Tell me.”

“Mercy is not something that can be forced. It drops like soft rain from heaven upon the place beneath it. It twice blesses: it blesses he who gives it and he who receives it. It is influential in the most influential people. It makes a king look better than his own crown does. His scepter shows his power and strength on earth, it is a credit to his awe and grandness. Within it sits the dread and fear of kings, but mercy has more power and is higher than the scepter. It is enthroned within the hearts of kings. It is a credit to God himself, earthly power seems most like God’s power when mercy is added to justice. So, Jew, although it is justice you want, consider this: following the course of justice alone won’t save you. We pray for mercy, and saying the prayer teaches us to give mercy. I have said all of this to persuade you to reduce the severity of your claim, which, if you follow through, this strict court of Venice will have to serve sentence against the merchant there.”

“My actions are my own! I want the law— the payment for the forfeit of the contract.”

“Can’t the contract just be dismissed with payment?”

"Yes, I'm willing to give it to him right here in the court," said Bassanio enthusiastically. It was the first thing the lawyer said that had given him hope. "Yes, even twice the amount, and if that is not enough I will sign a contract to pay it ten times over. I will give up my hands, my head, my heart. If that is not enough, it would seem you are just truly evil. I beg you, just once take the law into your authority— do a great right by doing a little wrong, and keep this devil from getting what he wants."

"No, that can't be," said the lawyer. "There is no power in Venice that can alter a law once it is established. It will be recorded as a precedent and many errors will occur by example as others rush in after it: it cannot be."

"A fine judge has come to judge!" said Shylock. "Yes, a Daniel! Oh, wise young judge—I do applaud you!"

"Please, let me look at the contract."

"Here it is, most respected expert, here it is." Shylock handed over the notarized paper.

"Shylock, they are offering you three times the amount you lent," said the lawyer with a surprise.

"But I made an oath! I made an oath by heaven! Should I have a false oath upon my soul? No, not for Venice."

"Well, this contract is forfeited. By law, this Jew may claim a pound of flesh to be cut off by him nearest the merchant's heart. But I'm asking you to show mercy: take three times the money, and let me tear up the contract."

"It can be torn up when it is paid according to its content. You do appear to be a worthy judge. You know the law well, and your argument has been very solid. I command you by the law— of which you are a well-deserving support of— yo make your judgment. By my soul I swear there is nothing anyone can say that will change my mind. I wait here for my payment."

"Please, I beg the court to give the judgment." Antonio had grown tired and wanted to rid himself the anticipation of death by accepting it.

"Well then, so it is: you must prepare your chest for his knife," the lawyer told Antonio.

"Oh, noble judge! Oh, excellent young man!" Shylock said.

"The law fully supports the penalty which is written in the contract."

"It's very true! Oh wise and upright judge! You seem much older than you look!"

"So, you must lay bare your chest."

“Yes, his chest: that’s what the contract says, doesn’t it, good judge? ‘Nearest his heart.’ Those are the words.”

“That is right. Is there a balance here to weight the flesh?”

“I have it ready,” Shylock motioned to a scale he had bought earlier from a butcher.

“Get a surgeon, Shylock, that you will pay to attend to his wounds and keep him from bleeding to death.”

“Does it say that in the contract?”

“It is not written in it, but so what? It would be good for you to show the charity.”

“I cannot find it—it is not in the contract.”

“You, merchant, do you have anything to say?”

"I don't have much to say," Antonio sighed. "I am ready and prepared. Give me your hand, Bassanio: goodbye! Don't be sad that I have fallen like this for you because Fortune is showing herself to be kinder than is her custom. She usually lets the man who has fallen low to outlive his wealth and to view with an empty eye and a wrinkled forehead the poverty that has set in, but as far as the lingering suffering and misery—Fortune has ended it. Speak well of me to your honorable wife. Tell her what happened to bring about my end and tell her I loved you, and speak well of me after I am gone. And when the story is told, allow her to be the judge of whether Bassanio once had a friend. Only feel sorry that you will lose your friend, and know he doesn't feel sorry to pay your debt. If the Jew cuts deep enough I will soon pay for it with all of my heart."

"Antonio," Bassanio said. "I have a wife who is as dear to me as life itself. But life itself, my wife, and all the world are not more important than your life. I would lose it all—yes—sacrifice them all to this devil, if I could save you."

"Your wife might not be happy to hear that, if she were here to hear you make that offer," said the lawyer.

"I have a wife whom I love very much," Gratiano said. "If she were in heaven, she could ask some heavenly power to change the mind of this dog Jew."

“It’s good you offer it behind her back,” said the clerk. “This wish would make for an argument at home.”

“That’s what you get with Christian husbands,” said Shylock. “I have a daughter. I’d rather any descendent of Barrabas would have been her husband instead of a Christian! But we're wasting time. Please, carry on with the sentence.”

“A pound of this merchant’s flesh is yours,” declared the lawyer. “The court awards it, and the law will give it to you.”

“You are a just judge!”

“And you must cut this flesh off of his chest. The law allows for it, and the court awards it.”

“You are an educated judge! A sentence! Come on, let’s get ready!” Shylock drew prepared the set of butcher's knives he had purchased along with the scale.

“Wait a minute. There is something else. This contract says that there should not be a spot of blood, the words say exactly ‘a pound of flesh.’ So, take your payment, and take your pound of flesh. But if, in cutting it, your shed one drop of Christian blood, your land and property are, by the law of Venice, confiscated to the state of Venice.”

“Oh, good judge! Listen, Jew! Oh, educated judge!” Gratiano became excited at the turn of events.

“Is that the law?” Shylock asked, distressed but not completely devoid of hope.

“You can look at it for yourself. You have asked for justice, and—rest assured— you will have more justice than you desired.”

“Oh, educated judge! Listen, Jew—an educated judge!” Gratiano continued.

Shylock paused. He knew he couldn't cut into Antonio without shedding blood. If the court was looking for the limits of Shylock's vengefulness, they had found it. “I will take your offer, then,” he said quietly. “Pay the principle three times over and let the Christian go free.” He waved his hand as if to dismiss the entire affair.

“Here is the money,” Bassanio prepared the ducats he had brought, relief spreading on his face and Antonio's.

“Wait!” the lawyer said. “The Jew wants justice. Wait! Don’t hurry. He will have nothing but his payment. So, prepare to cut off the flesh. Be careful not to shed any blood, or to cut more or less than exactly a pound of flesh. If you cut more or less than a pound—be it so little as to makes it lighter or heavier in weight by a twentieth of a part, even one ounce, if the scale shows but the weight of a hair — you die and all of your property will be confiscated.”

“A second Daniel! A very fair judge, Jew! Not, you who have no faith, I am one up on you.” Gratiano laughed.

“Why do you hesitate, Jew?” The lawyer said. “Take your payment.”

“Give me my principal, and I will go,” said Shylock.

“I have it ready for you,” said Bassanio. “Here it is.”

“He refused it in the open court,” the lawyer stopped Bassanio again. “He only wants justice and to have his payment.”

“So, I don’t even get my principal?” Shylock said.

“You will have nothing but the forfeiture, which will be taken at your risk, Jew.”

“Well, then the devil gives it to him! I won’t stay here any longer.” Shylock began packing his things.

"Wait a minute, Jew. The law still has a hold on you. It is written in the laws of Venice that if it be shown that a foreigner, by direct or indirect attempts, tries to take the life of a citizen of Venice, the person he tried to take the life of is entitled to one half of his property, and the other half goes to the state. The offender's life lies in the mercy of the duke, and only the duke. This seems to be your situation. It appears so, by clear course of action that you indirectly and directly taken. You have plotted against the life of the defendant, and you have, by your actions, brought on the harm to yourself I previously mentioned. So, get down on your knees, then, and beg mercy of the duke."

"Beg that you may be allowed to hang yourself," said Gratiano. "But, if your wealth goes to the state, you won't have enough money to buy a rope and you will have to be hung at cost to the state."

"I want you to see the difference between our temperaments," the duke spoke up, having watched the proceedings with interest. "I pardon your life before you ask for it. Half of your wealth goes to Antonio. The other half goes to the state. If you show humility, I may drop that to a fine."

"The state's half can be dropped, but not Antonio's," the lawyer said.

"No, go ahead and take my life with all of it," said Shylock. "Don't pardon that. You take my house when your take the income that keeps my house. You take my life when you take away the place where I live."

"Can you show him any mercy, Antonio?" the lawyer asked.

Antonio spoke up. "If the duke and the court drop the fine for one half of his property, I am satisfied; as long as he will allow the other half to be put in trust so that when he dies, it will go to the man who recently stole his daughter. And two more things: that he, due to this favor being granted, immediately becomes a Christian. The other is that he records a will, here in this court, that gives all when he dies to his son-in-law Lorenzo and his daughter."

The duke nodded his head. "He will do this or else I will take back the pardon I just gave to him."

"Are you happy with that, Jew? What do you say?" the lawyer asked Shylock.

"I am happy with that," responded Shylock. He wasn't, but at this point he didn't want to risk more punishment.

"Clerk, make up a deed of gift for him to sign."

"Please, allow me to leave now, I am not feeling well. Send the deed after me and I will sign it."

“Go on, then, but be sure to sign the deed,” the duke said.

Shylock left the court. He hadn't even bothered to take any of the butchering equipment he brought with him, leaving it on the floor and tables where he made his prosecution. The court audience applauded and headed out, with many congratulating Antonio and the lawyer who had managed to save the life of a fellow Venetian.

When the crowd cleared, the duke approached the lawyer. “Sir, please come to my house for dinner.”

“I humbly do request your pardon. I must leave tonight to go to Padua and it is urgent that I leave immediately.”

“I am sorry you don’t have the time to join me. Antonio, you should reward this gentleman. In my mind, you are very much in debt to him.” The duke left the court with the rest of the magnificoes.

Bassanio approached the lawyer and eagerly shook his hand. “Sir, my friend and I have been acquitted today due to your wisdom from serious penalties. We’d like to give you the three thousand ducats that were due the Jew as recompense for the pains you have taken on our behalf.”

“We would still be indebted to you and owe you love and service forever,” agreed Antonio.

“He who does a good job is well paid,” said the lawyer. “And I, in freeing you, am satisfied and I consider myself well paid in that alone. I wasn’t thinking about money. I hope you recognize me when we meet again. I wish you the best. I’m going to go, now.”

“Sir, I must insist you take some token from us, as a gift, not as a payment,” Bassanio insisted. “Please grant me two things: don’t say no, and forgive me for insisting.”

“You insist so much, and so I will give in and accept/” The lawyer stepped back, examined them, then spoke to Antonio. “Give me your gloves. I will wear them for your sake.” Antonio handed them without hesitation. “And from you,” the lawyer turned to Bassanio “that ring, I'll take it.” Bassanio hid the ring that he had promised Portia not to give away. “Don’t pull back your hand—I’ll have nothing else. You can’t deny me this gift.”

“But this ring, sir, it’s nothing! I would be ashamed to give you this.” Bassanio scrambled for excuses.

“I will having nothing else but the ring. Now that I think about it, I really want it.”

“This ring means more to me than its actual value. I will give you the most expensive ring in Venice, and put out a public announcement to find it. But please forgive me for not giving you this ring.”

"I see, sir, that you make big offers. You taught me how to beg, and now it seems you are teaching me how a beggar should be answered."

"Sir, this ring was given to me by my wife and when she put it on my finger she made me promise that I should never sell it or give it away or lose it."

"Many men use that excuse as a reason not to give things away. If your wife is not a madwoman and you told her how much I did to deserve the ring, she would not be mad at you forever for giving it to me." Bassanio didn't respond, hoping the lawyer would drop the topic. The lawyer merely smiled and shook the hands of Antonio and Bassanio. "Well, goodbye," the lawyer said before leaving with the clerk.

"Lord Bassanio," Antonio said, "let him have the ring. Consider how much he deserves and my friendship against your wife's order."

Bassanio let out a heavy sigh. "Go, Gratiano—run after him. Give him the ring and bring him, if you can, to Antonio's house. Hurry! Run after him!" Gratiano jetted took Bassanio's ring and jetted out of the court. "Come on, you and I will go now and early tomorrow morning we will both hurry to get to Belmont. Come on, Antonio."

Chapter 2

Dressed up as a lawyer and clerk respectively, Portia and Nerissa walked the streets of Venice with grins on their faces.

“Ask where the Jew’s house is, then give him this deed and have him sign it,” Portia told Nerissa. “We’ll leave tonight and be home a day before our husbands. Lorenzo will be happy to see this deed.”

The sound of running footsteps startled the girls, but they were calmed to see it was only Gratiano. “Sir, it’s a good thing I caught up with you. Bassanio took my advice and has sent me after you with this ring. He requests your company at dinner tonight.”

Portia regained her mannish impression. “We can’t do attend, but I accept his ring with much gratitude, so please tell him that. Also, Can you show this young man to Shylock’s house?”

“I will do that.” Gratiano began walking ahead.

“I’ll see if I can get my husband’s ring, which I made him swear to keep forever,” Nerissa said.

"I bet you will be able to. They will swear to us that they gave the rings to men, but we will confront then and swear more than them."

Part Five

Chapter 1

Lorenzo and Jessica walked through the garden on Portia's Belmont estate.

“The moon shines so brightly tonight,” said Antonio. “On a night like this, when the wind blows so gently in the treetops they barely make noise—on a night just like this, I think Troilus climbed the Troyan walls and sighed toward the Grecian tents where his love Cressida slept.”

“On a night like this Thisbe tripped over the dew when he saw the lion’s shadow before him and ran away in fear,” said Jessica.

“On a night like this, Dido stood with a willow branch in her hand on the wild seashore and signaled her lover to come back to Carthage.”

“On a night like this, Medea gathered the magic herbs that rejuvenated old Aeson.”

“On a night like this, Jessica stole from the wealthy Jew and with her spendthrift lover all the way to Belmont.”

“On a night like this young Lorenzo swore he loved Jessica very much and won her soul with many vows of love, but not one single vow was true.”

“On a night like this, pretty Jessica, like a troublesome person, said awful things about her lover, and he forgave her.”

“I would outdo you if making references to the night if nobody came, but, listen, I hear footsteps.”

A man approached the couple. “Who comes so quickly in the quiet of night?” asked Lorenzo.

“A friend,” the man responded.

“A friend! What friend? What is your name, please, friend?”

“My name is Stephano, and I am here to tell you my mistress will be here before the sun rises, back in Belmont. She’s still among the holy crosses at the monastery, where she’s on her knees praying for a happy marriage.”

“Who is coming with her?”

“Just a holy hermit and her maid. Tell me, has my master returned yet?”

“He’s not here, and we haven’t heard from him but let’s go inside, Jessica, and prepare a ceremony to welcome the mistress back to her house.”

Launcelot ran into the garden. “Hello! Hello! Wo, ha, ho! Hello! Hello!”

“Who’s shouting?” asked Lorenzo.

“Hello! Did you see Master Lorenzo? Master Lorenzo! Hello! Hello!”

“Stop the hollering, man, I’m here.”

Launcelot bumbled through the tall bushes. “Hello! Where? Where?”

“Here!”

Still unable to find the source of the voice, Launcelot just yelled out his news. “Tell him a message has arrived from my master, full of very good news. My master will be here before morning.”

“Sweetheart, let’s go in and wait for them to arrive. But, wait, it doesn’t matter—why should we go in? Friend Stephano, please make it known inside the house that your mistress is coming and bring musicians out here.”

Stephano left for the house.

“See how lovely the moonlight looks on the bank!” said Lorenzo. “Let’s sit here and let the sounds of music creep into our ears. The stillness of night time makes the music all the more sweet sounding. Sit down, Jessica. Look at how the floor of heaven is inlaid with a thin layer of bright gold: even the smallest star that you can see sings like an angel in its motion, silently choiring to the youthful cherubs. Immortal beings can hear the songs, but we who live here on earth and live in earthly bodies cannot hear it.”

The musicians came out of the house and prepared their instruments.

“Come on! Wake Diana with a song! With the sweetest touches play your instruments so your mistress can hear and bring her home with music.”

They obliged, and began a happy tune.

“I never feel like laughing when I hear sweet music,” said Jessica.

"That's because your feelings are paying attention to the music. Think about a frolicking herd of wild animals, or a herd of young and untrained colts jumping around like crazy, bellowing and neighing loudly, which is how they are naturally, but if they happen to hear the sound of a trumpet, or if the sound of soft music touches their ears, you will see them all stop and stand still— their wild eyes calming from the power of the music. That is why the poet wrote how Orpheus could bring trees, stones and rivers to him with music, there is not much in the world too stupid, hard or full of anger that can not be changed by music. The man that has no music in him— who is not moved by the harmony of sweet sounds— is only good for betrayal, schemes and ruin. His soul is as dull as the night and his emotions are dark as the son of Chaos. A man like that can not be trusted. Listen to the music."

Portia and Nerissa entered from the front of the house, hearing the music echo through the halls from the garden. "That light we see in burning in my house. Look how far that candle throws its beams! That's how a good deed shines in an evil world," said Portia.

"Brighter lights always dim the less. Another light shines as brightly as a king until the king comes along, and then the other light suddenly becomes less, in the same way an inland stream empties into the sea. Music! Listen!"

“It is your music, madam, coming from your house,” said Nerissa.

“I see now that you can’t consider anything good without comparison. I think music sounds sweeter at night than during the day.”

“The quiet of night gives it that quality, madam.”

“The crow sings as sweetly as the lark does when neither is listened to. I think the nightingale if it were to sing by day, when all the geese are cackling—would be no better regarded as a musician than the common wren. How many things are made to seem right and praised as perfect if they come at the right time! Quiet, now! The moon sleeps with its lover Endymion and will not be awoken.”

The music died down.

“That is the voice of Portia, if I am not mistaken,” Lorenzo said. He had heard the murmur of voices and told the musicians to stop their playing.

“He recognizes me like the blind man recognizes the cuckoo—by its bad voice.” Portia and Nerissa steeped forward, revealing themselves to the party.

“Dear lady, welcome home.”

"We have been praying for our husbands' health. We hope they are better off for our words. Have they come back, yet?"

"Madam, they are not back yet. But a messenger came earlier and said they are on their way."

"Go inside, Nerissa. Tell the servants they must not mention that we have been gone. You neither, Lorenzo, or you, Jessica."

The sound of a horn sounded from the front of the house.

"Your husband is here," said Lorenzo. "I hear his trumpet. We are not tattle-tales, madam, don't worry."

"I think this night looks like sick daylight," said Portia. "It looks a little paler. It's like a day when the sun is hidden."

Bassanio entered the garden, along with Antonio and Gratiano, as well as some servants.

"It is daylight on the other side of the world, while you walk here at night," said Bassanio.

"I will give light, as in joy, but I will not be light, as in promiscuous, since a wife who is light in that regard makes her husband heavy-hearted. Bassanio will never feel that way because of me, but God will sort it all out. Welcome home, my lord."

“Thank you, madam. Please welcome my friend. This is Antonio, who I told you about— the one I am forever indebted to.”

“You should in all senses of the word be indebted to him as I hear he was very much indebted to you.”

“I have been paid back for all of it very well,” spoke up Antonio.

“Sir, you are very welcome in our house. But what we see says more than words can, so I will cut this polite talk short:

Gratiano, who had taken Nerissa aside to speak to her, suddenly spoke up loudly. “By the moon in the sky I swear you’ve got it wrong. I really did give it to the judge’s clerk. He should have been castrated, as far as I’m concerned, for as much as it is upsetting you.”

“An argument already! What is the matter?”

“It’s about a hoop of gold, a trivial ring that she gave to me that had a little inscription on it that was nothing more that a knife-maker’s poem. It said: ‘Love me and don’t leave me.’”

"Are you talking about the inscription or the value?" Nerissa asked Gratiano. "You swore to me, when I gave it to you that you would wear it until you died, and that it would be buried with you in your grave. If not for me, then for the vows you made, you should have been respectful and kept it. You gave it to a judge's clerk! No, as God is my judge— the 'clerk' you gave it to will never grow hair on their face."

"He will if he lives to be a man."

"Right, if a woman lives to be a man."

"I swear by my hand, I gave it to a young man. Almost a boy, a little stubby boy— no taller than you—the judge's clerk, a boy who talked a lot and begged it as a fee. I couldn't find it in my heart to say no."

"I will speak plainly," Portia said, interrupting their bickering, "you were wrong. To so easily give away your wife's first gift— a thing stuck onto your finger with vows and fastened with faith to your flesh. I gave my lover a ring and made him swear never to part with it. Here he stands, and will be so bold to say he would not lose it or take it from his finger for all the wealth in the world. So, to be sure, Gratiano, you give your wife reason to grieve, and if it were me, I'd be angry, too."

"Bassanio gave his ring away, as well, to the judge that asked for it and did, to be certain, deserved it. Then the boy, his clerk, who took so much trouble in the writings—he wanted my ring, and neither man would take anything but the two rings."

"Which ring did you give, my lord? I hope it's not the one I gave to you."

Bassanio's face turned red. "If I could lie very well, I would deny it. But you can see my finger does not have a ring on it. It is gone."

"Your heart is empty of truth. By heaven, I will never come into your bed until I see that ring."

"I won't come into yours, either, until I see my ring again," agreed Nerissa.

"Sweet Portia," Bassanio said, "if you knew who I gave the ring to, and if you knew who I gave the ring for, and if you could guess how unwillingly I gave the ring, when nothing but the ring would be accepted, you would not be so unhappy with me."

“If you had realized the true value of the ring,” Portia said, “or half the worthiness of the one who gave you the ring, or your honor in keeping the ring— you would not have parted with the ring. What man is so unreasonable that if you had tried to defend the ring with any passionate feeling, lacked the restraint To stop pushing the issue? Nerissa shows me what to believe: I’ll die before some other woman had the ring.”

“No, trust me, madam, by my soul— I didn’t give it to a woman but to a doctor of law who refused to take three thousand ducats from me but begged for the ring, which I denied him and I felt bad about it seeing him go away unhappy. He had defended the very life of my dear friend. What can I say, sweet lady? I was compelled to send it to him. I was full of shame and in need of good manners. I could not dishonor him by not showing him gratitude— it would have made me feel bad. Forgive me, good lady. I swear, by these blessed candles that light the night, if you had been there, I think you would have begged me to give him the ring.”

"Don't let that legal expert come near my house. Since he has the jewel I loved, and which you did swear to keep for me, I will become as generous as you, and I will not deny him anything. No, not my body or my husband's bed. I will recognize him—I am sure of it. So, don't spend a night away from home. Watch me like Argus. If you don't I will be left alone and—by my word, which is still not mine— I will have that legal expert as my lover."

"And I will have his clerk," said Nerissa. "So be advised About leaving me to my own devices"

"Well if you do so, I'd better not catch him, then," said Gratiano. "If I do, I will damage the young clerk's pen."

"I am the reason for these arguments," spoke up Antonio, having watched the whole argument in anxious silence.

"Sir, don't worry—you are welcome despite all," responded Portia.

Bassanio continued his apologies. "Portia, forgive me this error I had to make. And, within hearing of all of these friends, I swear to you, by your beautiful eyes in which I see myself-"

"Make sure you hear that! In both my eyes he twice sees himself. In each eye, one, and so he's swearing by a double self. Well, that's a vow you can believe, isn't it?"

"No, listen to me— forgive me this time and I swear by my soul. That I will never again break a vow to you."

Antonio spoke up again. "I once lent my body for his wealth, which –without him who has your husband's ring— I would have lost. I'll risk being promised again and will give my soul upon forfeit, to guarantee that your lord, will not break a vow with awareness."

"Then you will be his guaranteer," Portia said. "Give him this and tell him to keep it better than the other." Portia handed him the ring that she had taken from Bassanio during her ruse.

"Here, Lord Bassanio—swear to keep this ring."

"Good lord, it is the same one I gave the legal expert!" Bassanio exclaimed.

"I got it from him," Portia said. "Forgive me, Bassanio, but I slept with the legal expert for this ring."

"And forgive me, my gentle Gratiano— the same stubby boy, the clerk, gave me this last night to sleep with him." Nerissa handed Gratiano the ring she had managed to take from him as the clerk.

"This is just like fixing roads in the summer when they are good enough," Gratiano said. "What, we get cheated on before we even deserve it?"

“Don’t speak so blatantly,” Portia said. “You are all dumbfounded. Here is a letter: read it slowly. It comes from Padua, from Bellario. In it you will find that Portia was the legal expert, and Nerissa was her clerk. Lorenzo will testify that I left the house as soon as you and just now returned. I haven’t even entered the house yet. Antonio, you are welcome here, and I have better news for you than you will expect. Open your letter soon and you will find that three of your ships have come into harbor, full of riches. I can not say by what strange chance I came upon this letter.”

Antonio took the letter and looked it over, unbelieving that what Portia had said was true. “I have no idea what to say.”

“You were the legal expert and I didn’t know it?” Bassanio asked.

“You were the clerk that is to cheat on me with my wife?” Gratiano asked.

“Yes, but the clerk will never be able to do it unless he grows to be a man,” Nerissa answered Gratiano.

“Sweet expert, you will be my bed-fellow,” Bassanio said. “When I am away, you can sleep with my wife.”

“Sweet lady, you have given me life and a reason to live, for here I read for certain that my ships are coming home safely,” said Antonio.

"Well, Lorenzo! My clerk has some comfort to offer to you, too," Portia said.

"Yes, and I will give them with no interest. Here, I give to you and Jessica a special deed of gift from the rich Jew which leaves you all he owns after he dies." Nerissa handed them the letter from her traveling bag.

Lorenzo smiled. "Beautiful ladies, you drop bread from heaven to starving people."

"It is almost morning," Portia said, "but I'm sure you are not yet satisfied with all of these events. Let's go inside and there you can ask us questions and we will answer all things truthfully."

"Let's do that," Gratiano said. "My first question for Nerissa to be sworn to answer is whether she would rather wait until tomorrow night or go to bed now, with only two hours left until morning. If the day were to come, I would wish it was still dark, and that I were sleeping with the expert's clerk. Well, as long as I live I'll fear nothing else as much as I will fear keeping Nerissa's ring safe."

Printed in Great Britain
by Amazon